Response to Intervention in MATH

Response to Intervention in MATH

Paul J. Riccomini

Bradley S. Witzel

CORWIN

A SAGE Company

For information:

Corwin
A SAGE Company
2455 Teller Road
Thousand Oaks, California 91320
(800) 233-9936
Fax: (800) 417-2466
www.corwin.com

SAGE India Pvt. Ltd.
B 1/I 1 Mohan Cooperative Industrial Area
Mathura Road, New Delhi 110 044
India

SAGE Ltd.
1 Oliver's Yard
55 City Road
London EC1Y 1SP
United Kingdom

SAGE Asia-Pacific Pte. Ltd.
33 Pekin Street #02-01
Far East Square
Singapore 048763

Printed in the United States of America

Library of Congress Cataloging-in-Publication Data

Riccomini, Paul J.
Response to intervention in math/Paul J. Riccomini and Bradley S. Witzel.
    p. cm.
Includes bibliographical references and index.
ISBN 978-1-4129-6635-1 (pbk.)

    1. Mathematics—Study and teaching (Elementary) 2. Mathematics—Study and teaching (Middle school) 3. Effective teaching. 4. Curriculum planning. 5. Learning disabled children—Education. 6. Mathematical ability—Testing. I. Witzel, Bradley S. II. Title.

QA135.6.R53 2010
372.7—dc22   2009035719

This book is printed on acid-free paper.

10   11   12   13   14   10   9   8   7   6   5   4   3   2

Acquisitions Editor:	David Chao
Editorial Assistant:	Sarah Bartlett
Production Editor:	Jane Haenel
Copy Editor:	Cheryl Rivard
Typesetter:	C&M Digitals (P) Ltd.
Proofreader:	Susan Schon
Indexer:	Terri Corry
Cover and Graphics Designer:	Michael Dubowe

Contents

Preface

PURPOSE OF THIS BOOK

The purpose of this book is to introduce the overarching principles of an effective response to intervention (RTI) framework in mathematics with the primary focus on instructional recommendations for teachers to improve their day-to-day instruction in mathematics. More and more schools, school districts, and state departments of education continue to expand current RTI models in reading to mathematics to help struggling students. Teachers and administrators are seeking guidance on how best to teach mathematics to students who are struggling and/or have learning disabilities. The eventual result of any effective RTI model is to increase the number of students successful (e.g., increased proficiency) in the general education mathematics classroom, Tier 1. This book is designed to provide instructional recommendations for teaching mathematics effectively to students who have traditionally struggled and draws upon currently available research-based evidence for teaching mathematics.

The National Mathematics Advisory Panel's (NMAP) final report, *Foundations for Success* (2008), clearly states that effective mathematical programs must simultaneously develop (a) conceptual understanding, (b) computational fluency, (c) factual knowledge, and (d) problem-solving skills if students are to be successful in more advanced mathematics courses (e.g., algebra and geometry). Additionally, the NMAP (2008) specifically addresses the instructional needs of low-achieving students, students who struggle, and students with learning disabilities and provides instructional recommendations for teaching these groups of students. The Institute of Education Sciences (IES) released a Practice Guide, *Assisting Students Struggling With Mathematics: Response to Intervention (RTI) for Elementary and Middle Schools*, which puts forth nine recommendations to effectively deliver a math RTI model. Therefore, the recommendations contained in this book will address each of the areas highlighted in the NMAP's *Final Report* (2008) and the IES Practice Guide (2009) with the intent to provide instructionally relevant recommendations and assist educators who are responsible for improving the mathematics programs for students who are underperforming, struggling, and/or have learning disabilities.

TARGET AUDIENCE OF THIS BOOK

One only has to look at a publisher's catalog to see the overwhelming number of RTI books for teachers and administrators; the list may total in the hundreds. Not surprisingly, almost all the published materials focus exclusively on the process (e.g., procedures and assessment) of setting up and implementing RTI models in reading; mathematics, if addressed at all, is given a cursory mention. We certainly recognize the importance of reading, because if students are unable to read at a functional level, they will struggle in many academic areas, including mathematics. However, mathematics education deserves a reform focused on student performance. That said, this book is written for any educator charged with the responsibility of teaching mathematics, particularly those who teach struggling students.

With the emergence of RTI at all levels, school accountability, and emphasis on preparing more students for algebra, the primary responsibility for addressing the instructional needs of *all* students is placed squarely on the shoulders of general education mathematics teachers: elementary and secondary. We contend that if the instructional strategies and recommendations contained in this book are systematically incorporated into the general education mathematics day-to-day classroom instruction, the more likely *all* students will be successful.

We are certainly aware of the realities of the education system and recognize that much of the responsibility of teaching struggling learners within an RTI model often falls at the feet of special educators, curriculum coaches, interventionists, and even school psychologists. This book is also written for those of you who act in the capacity of supporting the general education teacher (e.g., coteaching, resource teachers, tutors) and/or delivering targeted interventions. Additionally, parents of young children are now both experiencing firsthand the shortfalls within their children's elementary mathematics programs and having to address these shortfalls with their children. We hope many parents who read this book find the information helpful as they research ideas to support their children's mathematical development.

WHY IS THE BOOK NEEDED?

Teaching mathematics effectively requires skillful planning and a deep understanding of not only mathematical concepts but also effective instructional pedagogy, especially when teaching students who are low achievers, struggling, and/or have learning disabilities. The NMAP's *Final Report* (2008) states unequivocally that research over many years clearly indicates that students who are low achievers and struggling to learn mathematics and/or have learning disabilities require regular access to explicit methods of instruction available on a regular basis. This conclusion, although evidenced by data, has been scrutinized by some people in education. As more and more students with learning disabilities and other significant instructional needs are being included in the general education mathematics classroom, general education teachers are being required to more effectively meet struggling students' many and varied needs in the context of their daily instructional lessons. As researchers, we support the implementation of evidence-supported practices to the maximum extent possible and focus our recommendations in this book accordingly. As parents, we applaud the teachers who do the same in their classrooms.

Response to Intervention in Math provides educators with an understanding of the components of effective instructional design and delivery for students with diverse needs in the area of mathematics. Specifically, readers will learn procedures for teaching mathematics using systematic and explicit instruction as an approach to assessment, instructional planning, and evaluation. The instructional recommendations found in this book are aligned with the recommendations put forth by the NMAP's *Final Report* (2008; www.ed.gov/mathpanel), the IES Practice Guide written by Gersten and Colleagues (2009), and the research base on effective mathematics instruction, albeit relatively small compared to research available for reading.

The authors would also like to note that there is no one "thing" or "waving of a magic mathematics wand" that will address the many and varied issues impacting the learning or lack of learning in mathematics. Specific student differences are so widely diverse and often very complex, it is unlikely that the ideas in this book will address every student issue appearing in classrooms. As such, none of the recommendations in this book should be interpreted as "absolutes," but rather as starting points for consideration in the context of your mathematics program and specific characteristics of your students. Moreover, we advocate that only a concerted effort at all levels and by all educators, both general and special education teachers, is an effective and efficient approach that will ultimately capitalize on efforts to improve your school's curriculum and instruction in the area of mathematics. Without unilateral support for student learning and improvements in mathematics, an RTI math effort is premature.

CHAPTER OVERVIEW

Chapter 1, "What Is RTI, and Why Is It Important?" provides an overview of response to intervention (RTI) in general and how it specifically relates to teaching mathematics. Topics covered in this chapter include an overview and description of RTI practices and procedures and common components in models of RTI, and it concludes with a brief overview of key research supporting RTI in mathematics.

Chapter 2, "The RTI Process for Math," provides a description of the essential components to consider when designing and implementing an RTI model in math, more detailed description of the standard protocol model and problem-solving model, progress monitoring, and the importance of the core mathematics program.

Chapter 3, "A Tiered Approach to More Effective Mathematics Instruction," differentiates different levels of instruction and intervention necessary for implementing RTI. Additionally, through a series of detailed self-studies of curriculum, instructional delivery, and interventions along with some classroom examples, it becomes evident whether a school or district is ready to initiate RTI in mathematics.

Chapter 4, "Mathematics Interventions Overview," describes who requires interventions and how to define the necessary interventions per each student's needs. Details about building an appropriate environment for interventions as well as choosing effective curriculum and instructional delivery are explained as well as setting the time frame for intervention and developing interventions. The chapter includes a list of mathematics interventions and programs to consider.

Chapter 5, "Number Sense and Initial Math Skills," details the basic components of number sense and early numeracy as defined by educational programs and related assessments. More important, from number recognition, to magnitude, to counting strategies for basic facts, instruction delivery and interventions are described, with illustrations that may be used to teach number sense to students who are struggling in mathematics.

Chapter 6, "Building Students' Proficiency With Whole Numbers," provides a rationale for the importance of teaching students to proficiency with basic whole number operations. Instructional strategies will be provided for building understanding, relationships, and fluency with whole numbers. Peer-assisted learning strategies (PALS) in math are also described for kindergarten and Grades 2–6.

Chapter 7, "Fractions and Decimals," acknowledges the major struggles that students have with fractions, decimals, and percents. These struggles are worse for those with math difficulties. The failure to succeed in fractions has an ill effect on performance in secondary mathematics, particularly algebra. In this chapter, grade-level expectations are set along with illustrated ways on how to instruct and intervene with the teaching of fractions.

Chapter 8, "Teaching Problem Solving Strategically," will present teaching problem solving strategically through three problem-solving programs that have been used as Tier 2 instructional programs.

Chapter 9, "The Importance of Teaching Mathematical Vocabulary," focuses exclusively on mathematical vocabulary and how it influences mathematical proficiency. Five general guidelines for teaching vocabulary and seven math-specific recommendations for teaching mathematical vocabulary are described. Additionally, five instructional activities to facilitate deeper understanding are described and how to assess student's vocabulary knowledge.

Chapter 10, "Next Steps in the RTI Process," explores the next steps as models continue to be refined and expanded to secondary settings, other student groups such as gifted and talented, and implications for changing systems. Additionally, an alternative approach to Tier 1 instructional programs is described for future consideration.

Acknowledgments

Corwin gratefully acknowledges the contributions of the following individuals:

Rachel Aherns, Level 1 Special Education/Sixth-Grade Collaboration
  Teacher
West Des Moines Community School District
West Des Moines, IA

David Allsopp, Professor
Department of Special Education
University of South Florida
Tampa, FL

Judith Filkins, K–8 Math Curriculum Coordinator
Lebanon School District
Lebanon, NH

Russell Gersten, Professor Emeritus
Executive Director
College of Education Instructional Research Group
University of Oregon
Eugene, OR

Kent Johnson, Founder and Director
Morningside Academy
Seattle, WA

About the Authors

Paul J. Riccomini, PhD, began his career as a dual-certified general education mathematics teacher of students with learning disabilities, emotional and behavioral disabilities, and gifted and talented students in Grades 7–12 in inclusive classrooms. His teaching experiences required a strong content knowledge in mathematics and the development and maintenance of strong collaborative relationships with both general and special educators. He earned his doctorate in special education from The Pennsylvania State University and his master's degree in education and Bachelor of Arts in mathematics at Edinboro University of Pennsylvania. Currently, he is an Associate Professor of Special Education at Clemson University. His research focus is on effective instructional approaches, strategies, and assessments for students who are low achievers and/or students with learning disabilities in mathematics. He has written several research and practitioner articles related to effective strategies for teaching mathematics to students who struggle and has coauthored two math intervention programs targeting fractions and integers. As a former middle and high school general education and special education mathematics teacher, Dr. Riccomini knows firsthand the challenges and difficulties teachers experience every day when working with struggling students, a motivation for writing this book. You can e-mail Dr. Riccomini at pjr146@clemson.edu.

Bradley S. Witzel, PhD, is an experienced and decorated teacher of students with disabilities and at-risk concerns. He has worked as a classroom teacher and before that as a paraeducator in inclusive and self-contained settings. Dr. Witzel received his BS in psychology from James Madison University and his master's degree in education and his PhD in special education from the University of Florida. He currently serves as an associate professor, coordinator of the three special education programs, and assistive department chair of curriculum and instruction at Winthrop University in Rock Hill, South Carolina, where he recently received the 2009 Winthrop Graduate Faculty Award. In higher education, Dr. Witzel has taught undergraduate and graduate courses in special and general education methods as well as a variety of other courses from transition to behavior support. He has written several research and practitioner articles, books, and book chapters on mathematics education and interventions, and served as a reviewer of the Final Report from the National Mathematics Advisory Panel. Recently he coauthored an IES practice guide on response to intervention in mathematics. You can e-mail Dr. Witzel at witzelb@winthrop.edu.

What Is RTI, and Why Is It Important?

1

The main objective of RTI is not to identify students for special education but rather to help all students achieve at a proficient level and ultimately make adequate yearly progress.

—Carla Osberg, Nebraska Department of Education

I t has been 5 years since the passage of the reauthorization of IDEA and almost 8 years since the No Child Left Behind Act became law, and educators are still struggling with the reality of evidenced-based instructional practices and response to intervention (RTI) as an alternative means for helping struggling students as well as identifying those who qualify for special education services. This book is about how to improve mathematics instruction for all students within an RTI framework with a primary focus on elementary and middle school students.

We begin by providing a brief overview of what RTI is and how it is currently being implemented, but the majority of this book will focus almost exclusively on how to design and deliver more effective mathematics instruction. Topics covered in this chapter include an overview and description of RTI practices and procedures and common components in models of RTI, and it concludes with a brief overview of key research supporting RTI in mathematics. The remaining chapters in the book will focus on essential mathematics content and instructional strategies to better facilitate the learning of struggling students.

OVERVIEW OF RTI

Response to intervention (RTI) is the process by which schools improve learning through evidenced-based instruction, assessment, and interventions. Although educators have been working expeditiously over the past several years to design, develop, refine, and implement RTI models to improve instruction, the process and sometimes progress are painfully slow and continuously interrupted. It is not our intent to redefine or reconceptualize or even justify RTI for the field of education, but rather to focus on the instructional implementation of RTI in mathematics.

Various models, definitions, and procedures exist across the country regarding RTI models and frameworks. There is not necessarily one absolute definition or set of procedures to implement an effective RTI model. For example, in 2007 the Division for Learning Disabilities (DLD) described three common variables that impact RTI approaches:

> In general, RTI approaches depend upon (a) implementation in general education of instruction and interventions that are based on sound research, (b) assessment of students' response to these interventions, and (c) use of the assessment data to make decisions about whom to serve and whether to continue current forms of instruction or employ other methods and techniques. (DLD, 2007, p. 3)

The National Association of State Directors of Special Education (NASDSE, 2006) define eight core principles of response to intervention that capture the most important aspects of RTI and overlap with the 2007 DLD description of RTI. In the document *Response to Intervention: Policy Considerations and Implementation* (2006), the eight core principles identified include the following:

1. We can effectively teach all children.

2. Intervene early.

3. Use a multitier model of service delivery.

4. Use a problem-solving model to make decisions within a multitier model.

5. Use scientific, research-based validated intervention and instruction to the extent available.

6. Monitor student progress to inform instruction.

7. Use data to make decisions. A data-based decision regarding student response to intervention is central to RTI practices.

8. Use assessment for screening, diagnostics, and progress monitoring.

Many definitions of RTI exist in education; however, several common principles across each and every RTI model are apparent and have helped shaped the guiding principles for this book. Although RTI can have many meanings depending on your professional role in the school system, for the purposes of this book, RTI will comprise six guiding principles (Table 1.1):

1. **Belief System** that is founded on the idea that all students can learn when appropriate and effective instruction is provided and monitored. All educators understand that the purpose of RTI is to improve learning for all students and is not to identify more students for special education services. Moreover, general education teachers and special education recognize the shared responsibility required for RTI to be effective.

2. **Universal Screening** is utilized to measure all students' progress at least three to four times a year and identify those students in need of more intensive instruction. The screening measures are relatively short and simple to administer and are demonstrated to be technically adequate (i.e., reliable and valid measures of student learning). Both regular and special education teachers are vested in the use of assessment data for instructional decisions.

3. **Progress Monitoring** becomes a valued and important part of day-to-day instructional decisions made by classroom teachers. Progress monitoring of struggling students is standard practice by all teachers, and both programs and instructional interventions are evaluated based on student progress. Teachers recognize that assessment is important but useless if it is not used to inform instructional decisions.

4. **Research-Based Interventions** become the foundation of the core instructional program as well as interventions used in the different instructional tiers. Decisions regarding programs and interventions are based on high-quality research evidence and not on teachers' philosophy or personal beliefs about learning; interventions are selected based on student instructional needs, learning characteristics, and content.

5. **Instructional Tiers** are a systematic and carefully designed instructional system and are in place with all educators completely familiar with the model. An effective instructional tier system requires continuous communication and collaboration among all teachers involved with instruction and assessment. Each tier of instruction is closely aligned and instruction becomes more teacher directed and explicit as students move up through the tiers. Core instructional programs, instructional delivery, and interventions are based on high-quality research when available.

6. **Ongoing Evaluation and Refinement Procedures** are essential to the continued improvement of RTI procedures. Teachers recognize the importance of implementing with fidelity the assessments, instructional programs, and interventions selected for the RTI model being used, and procedures exist for evaluating the level of fidelity. It is also important for educators to be aware of the importance of refining RTI procedures year to year to maximize resources and effectiveness.

Table 1.1 Six Guiding Principles for RTI Models	
Steps	*Description*
1	Belief System
2	Universal Screening
3	Progress Monitoring
4	Research-Based Interventions
5	Instructional Tiers
6	Ongoing Evaluation and Refinement Procedures

The following sections will provide a brief overview of assessment, instructional tiers, and a summary of key research applying RTI models to mathematics. Later chapters in this book will cover each area in more depth and detail.

Assessment

Because the purpose of RTI is to improve student learning by improving instructional supports and interventions, assessment is pivotal for any RTI model in math. Assessment in an RTI model is very different than the assessments teachers are accustomed to using in their classrooms. Teachers generally use skill-based, criterion-referenced tests at the end of each unit or chapter to measure student learning on the specific content covered. This serves a variety of purposes including grade determination and evaluation of learning of specific content. Assessments in the context of an RTI model are very different and include three types: (1) universal screening, (2) progress monitoring, and (3) diagnostic assessment. No matter the type of assessment, the results are used for data-based decisions regarding instructional effectiveness, student progress, and areas requiring further instruction (see Table 1.2). A more detailed description of math assessments is provided in Chapter 2.

Table 1.2 Type and Purpose of Assessment in an RTI Math Model		
Type	*Frequency*	*Purpose*
Universal Screening	All students 3–4 times/year	Assessment is used for initial determination of which students are making adequate progress in their math performance at expected rates of improvement, and for identifying which students are needing additional interventions and more frequent progress monitoring to keep pace with the learning rates of typically achieving peers.
Progress Monitoring	Struggling students 1–4 times/month	Short and frequent skill-based, ongoing assessments that are sensitive to small changes in student learning; used to determine if the math instruction and/or interventions are significantly improving student learning across time. Data are generally disabled graphically.
Diagnostic Assessment	Students not responding to Tier 1 or Tier 2 instructional supports	Provides teachers with more in-depth and specific information about students' skills and instructional needs to plan specific interventions. Usually much longer in length and administered by an individual with special training on the diagnostic assessment.
Data-Based Decision Making	Ongoing	Continued analysis of student progress monitoring data to guide day-to-day instructional adjustments; provides information used to improve instruction, evaluate effectiveness, and determine students' need for more instruction.

Source: Adapted from the Presenters Guide: *Leaving No Child Behind: Response to Intervention: Fundamentals for educators and their partners.* Retrieved August 15, 2008, from www.ideapartnership.org, p. 27.

Instructional Tiers

RTI models include a system of instructional tiers; generally, three tiers are the most common system, but four tiers of instructional support are also being utilized. As students move through the tiers, instructional supports and interventions become more intensive. The tiers serve the purpose of structuring instructional supports with the goal of intervening early in the school year to prevent students from requiring special education services (see Figure 1.1). The following section provides an overview of a system of instructional tiers. We provide more detail on a tiered approach for math in Chapter 3.

Tier 1 is generally referred to as the core instructional program. In most states, this core program is determined by state standards and delivered through a commercially available mathematics curriculum. Tier 1 instruction should be effective for the majority of the student population. Most models suggest effectiveness for 80% of the students. This is an ambitious goal and will require Tier 1 teachers to differentiate and provide additional instructional supports to students who are struggling prior to moving these students into Tier 2 instructional supports.

Tier 2 instruction is generally described as more intensive and explicit than instruction in Tier 1. Usually, in Tier 2 instructional time is added to the instructional time in Tier 1. Although no specific recommendations for allocated math

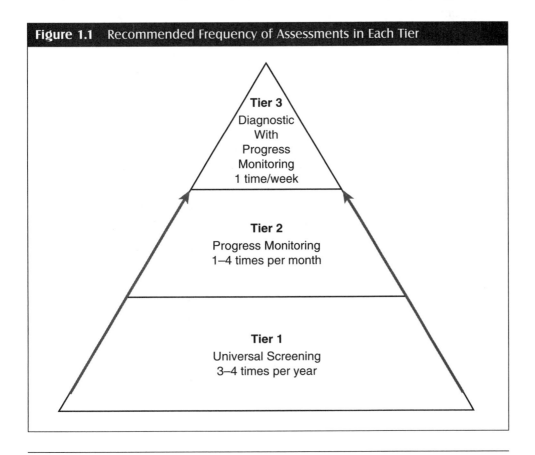

Figure 1.1   Recommended Frequency of Assessments in Each Tier

Tier 3
Diagnostic
With
Progress
Monitoring
1 time/week

Tier 2
Progress Monitoring
1–4 times per month

Tier 1
Universal Screening
3–4 times per year

Note: As students move up through the tiers, progress monitoring must occur more frequently to better facilite instructional decisions in a timely fashion.

time are found in the research, we recommend that Tier 1 instruction be a minimum of 50–60 minutes per day with an additional 20–30 minutes in Tier 2 for students who are struggling.

Tier 3 is generally described as the most intensive instruction and is reserved for students who have received evidenced-based instruction and various levels of intensity in Tiers 1 and 2 but have still not made adequate progress or have made no progress. At this point, the RTI team may decide that the students in the very top of the instructional pyramid require a different core program, one that is much more intensive, systematic, and explicit. If the effectiveness of Tier 1 and Tier 2 instruction is maximized, no more than 5% of the student population should require services in Tier 3 (see Figure 1.2).

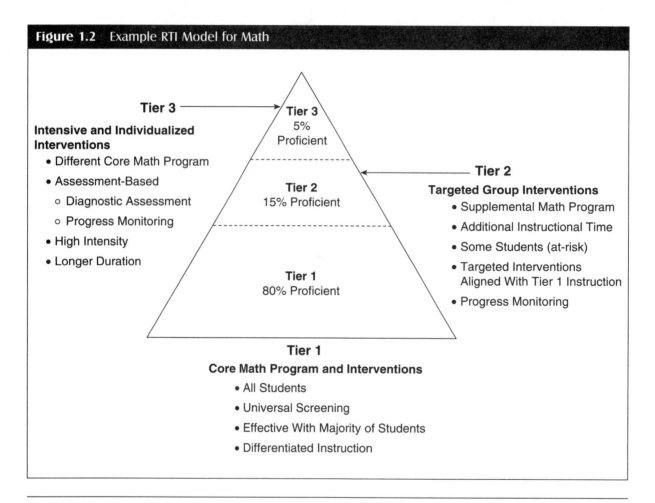

Figure 1.2 Example RTI Model for Math

Tier 3 ⟶ **Tier 3**
5%
Proficient

Intensive and Individualized Interventions
- Different Core Math Program
- Assessment-Based
  - Diagnostic Assessment
  - Progress Monitoring
- High Intensity
- Longer Duration

Tier 2
15% Proficient

Tier 2
Targeted Group Interventions
- Supplemental Math Program
- Additional Instructional Time
- Some Students (at-risk)
- Targeted Interventions Aligned With Tier 1 Instruction
- Progress Monitoring

Tier 1
80% Proficient

Tier 1
Core Math Program and Interventions
- All Students
- Universal Screening
- Effective With Majority of Students
- Differentiated Instruction

Note: The dashed lines separating the instructional tiers indicate that students can move back and forth from each instructional tier depending on student progress. Generally, Tier 2 instructional supports are in addition to Tier 1. In other words, students receiving Tier 2 instruction remain in the Tier 1 core math program. Also, three tiers of instructional supports are most common, but some RTI models have four tiers.

KEY RESEARCH SUPPORT FOR RTI AND MATHEMATICS

As educators continue to refine and expand RTI to mathematics, it is important that decisions are guided by the best available research. Unfortunately, to date the majority of research conducted on RTI models is in the area of reading and generally at the elementary levels. As more and more schools expand RTI to mathematics, more research will be conducted, thus providing more guidance on the best practices for RTI in mathematics.

This section provides a brief overview of a report titled *A Summary of Nine Key Studies: Multitier Intervention and Response to Interventions for Students Struggling in Mathematics*, from the Center on Instruction (www.centeroninstruction .org). The reason we are reviewing these particular studies is that the Center on Instruction goes to great lengths in determining the quality of research; hence, the studies selected for review are rigorous, experimental studies of the highest quality, a gold standard for research, that focus on a response to intervention framework to help students who are struggling to learn mathematics (Newman-Gonchar, Clarke, & Gersten, 2009) (see Table 1.3).

Eight overarching principles for an effective RTI framework in mathematics emerged from the research and include (1) increased instructional time and supports, (2) small-group instruction, (3) explicit methods of instruction, (4) the use of concrete and pictorial representations, (5) strategy instruction for problem solving, (6) focusing on basic facts and word problems, (7) aligning instruction from Tier 1 with Tier 2 to maximize the effectiveness, and (8) screening and progress monitoring to focus instruction on deficit areas. Professionals responsible for designing and implementing an RTI framework for students struggling with mathematics must carefully consider these principles that have materialized from the research. A brief description of each principle is provided below.

Increased Instructional Time and Supports

Consistent in almost all RTI models is increasing instructional time for students who are struggling. Generally, each tier of an RTI model includes an increase in instructional time. Teachers should make every effort to provide additional instructional time and engagement in the core mathematics program, Tier 1, before and after students have moved into Tier 2. Although all RTI models provide increased instructional time as students move through the tiers, no specific amount of time has been clearly identified in the research (see Figure 1.3 on p. 10).

The additional instructional time provided in the studies reviewed ranged from 5 minutes to 30 minutes per day. We recommend that students should spend at least 50–60 minutes per day in the core mathematics program, and students who struggle should receive at least 20–30 minutes of additional instruction every day. A student who is identified as struggling in mathematics could receive as much as 70–90 minutes of mathematics instruction per day for a period of at least 4–6 weeks. Students who fail to make adequate progress in Tier 1 and Tier 2 will move into a Tier 3 support. Depending on the student's age and deficits, Tier 3 could require the use of a corrective intensive mathematics program for at least 60 minutes per day. Increasing instructional time can result in increased levels of student achievement and possibly reduce the number of students requiring special education services.

Table 1.3 Summary of Key Research Involving RTI Models and Mathematics Performance

Citation	Participants	Math Content	Tier	Intervention	Results
Ardoin, Witt, Connell, & Koenig, 2001	14 4th-grade students	Two-digit subtraction with regrouping	Tiers 1 & 2	STEEP Tier 1: 14-minute classwide intervention with teacher modeling and peer tutoring; Tier 2: 20-minute peer-tutoring practice activity	Classwide intervention increased mean achievement scores on subtraction problems; Tier 2: 4 of 5 students increased their mean scores compared to baseline.
Bryant, Bryant, Gersten, Scammacca, & Chavez, 2008	266 1st- & 2nd-grade students	Number, number operations, and quantitative reasoning	Tier 2	15-minute intervention in addition to core math 3–4 times per week for 18 weeks; small group	Significant positive improvement for 2nd-grade students; overall achievement for 1st- & 2nd-grade students still below typically achieving peers.
Fuchs, Compton, Fuchs, Paulsen, Bryant, & Hamlett, 2005	564 2nd-grade students; 42% free & reduced lunch	Number and number operations	Tier 2	40-minute intervention in addition to core math; small group	Significant positive impact on at-risk students' scores; performance gap still existed.
Fuchs, Fuchs, & Hollenbeck, 2007	3rd-grade students	Word problem solving	Tiers 1 & 2	Hot Math Curriculum; 25–40 minutes for a total of 32 lessons in addition to core math; small group	Students receiving Hot Math in Tier 1 significantly reduced rate of "unresponsiveness" to 55% & 62%; students in Tier 1 and Tier 2 significantly reduced rate of "unresponsiveness" to 12% & 26%.
Fuchs et al. (in press)	1,141 3rd-grade students; 54.9% free & reduced lunch	Complex word problems	Tiers 1 & 2	SBI in small group aligned with content covered in Tier 1	Number of students at risk for mathematics disabilities decreased significantly with SBI tutoring across 4 years.

Citation	Participants	Math Content	Tier	Intervention	Results
Fuchs, Fuchs, & Prentice, 2004	201 3rd-grade students; 50% free & reduced lunch	Multistep word problems	Tier 1	Hot Math Curriculum; 25–40 minutes for a total of 32 lessons in addition to core math; small group	Overall improvement; students at risk for MD improved less; students with MD & RD improved the least.
Fuchs, Seethaler, Powell, Fuchs, Hamlett, & Fletcher, 2008	42 3rd-grade students below 36th percentile of WRAT & T score above 36th percentile on WASI	Word problems	Tier 2	One-one-one; 20–30 minutes 3 times per week for 12 weeks in addition to core math	Mixed results; positive on researcher-created measures; not significant on key mathematics and ITSB problem subtests.
VanDerHeyden & Burns, 2005	3rd–5th-grade students	Computation and recall of basic facts	Tiers 1 & 2	Tier 1: 30-minute/day classwide peer tutoring; Tier 2: 5-minute additional teacher-led instruction	Improved standardized score of proficient students, but very little change of students scoring below average prior to intervention.
VanDerHeyden, Witt, & Gilbertson, 2007	2,708 elementary students	Computational speed and accuracy	Tiers 1 & 2	STEEP; Tier 1 included 10 minutes/day for 10 days; Tier 2 students received an additional 10 minutes of tutoring	Teachers requested fewer children be evaluated; those students referred for further evaluation were more likely to be eligible.

Notes: STEEP: Screening to Enhance Equitable Educational Placement; SBI: Schema-Broadening Instruction.

Source: Adapted from Newman-Gonchar, R., Clarke, B., & Gersten, R. (2009). *A summary of nine key studies: Multitier intervention and response to interventions for students struggling in mathematics.* Portsmouth, NH: RMC Research Corporation, Center on Instruction.

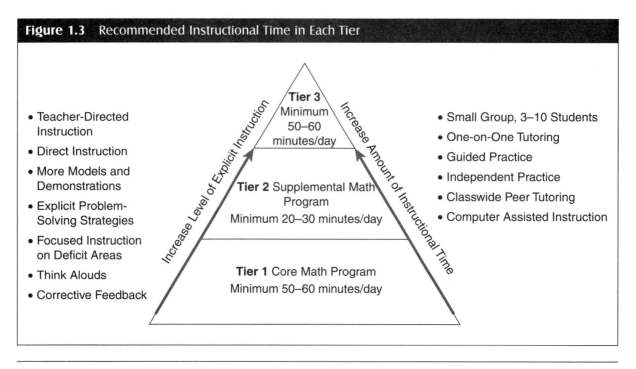

Figure 1.3 Recommended Instructional Time in Each Tier

- Teacher-Directed Instruction
- Direct Instruction
- More Models and Demonstrations
- Explicit Problem-Solving Strategies
- Focused Instruction on Deficit Areas
- Think Alouds
- Corrective Feedback

Increase Level of Explicit Instruction

Increase Amount of Instructional Time

Tier 3 Minimum 50–60 minutes/day

Tier 2 Supplemental Math Program
Minimum 20–30 minutes/day

Tier 1 Core Math Program
Minimum 50–60 minutes/day

- Small Group, 3–10 Students
- One-on-One Tutoring
- Guided Practice
- Independent Practice
- Classwide Peer Tutoring
- Computer Assisted Instruction

Note: As students move through the tiers, instructional time and level of instructional explicitness must be increased.

Small-Group Instruction

All the studies reviewed moved students into smaller groups when delivering Tier 2 instruction/intervention. Small-group instruction is defined as fewer than 10 students but most often involves 3–5 students. When considering the size of instructional groups, consider the number of students needing additional instruction and the number of highly qualified teachers available. Maximize the resources available; if instruction can be effective in groups of 5–10 students, then more students can receive additional instructional time if one-on-one tutoring is employed.

Grouping for instruction can facilitate teachers' ability to provide more and better individualized instruction, more opportunities for students to respond and actively engage in learning, and increase on-task behavior of students. As students move through the tiers, instructional groups should be smaller, thereby allowing teachers to maximize the effectiveness of their instruction. It is also imperative that instructional grouping is utilized by the Tier 1 teacher; whole-class instruction all the time will not allow for teachers to individualize instruction based on student needs. Tier 1 teachers should use a combination of whole-class instruction with small-group instruction, thereby not only allowing additional instruction for students who are struggling but also enriching or accelerating students who are not struggling.

Explicit Methods of Instruction

In all nine studies, instruction became more systematic and explicit as students moved into Tier 2 interventions. For students who are struggling, teachers are more effective if their presentation of mathematical concepts and/or skills is systematic and explicit. The National Mathematics Advisory Panel (NMAP, 2008) recommends that students who are low achieving, at risk for mathematical difficulties, and/or have learning disabilities must have regular access to explicit methods of instruction. Students moving into Tier 2 should have instruction that is more explicit and teacher directed than instruction in Tier 1. Additionally, students must have the opportunity to receive explicit teacher-led instruction during the core mathematics program in Tier 1 before moving into Tier 2.

The NMAP's final report (2008) went on to state very clearly that effective mathematics instruction includes opportunities for both student-centered and teacher-directed instruction. Exclusive use of either approach is not supported by research (NMAP, 2008). The NMAP's (2008) recommendations should also impact schools' decision-making processes for selection of the core mathematics program. Certain programs are designed around one instructional approach (i.e., student centered or teacher directed), whereas other programs attempt to balance instruction with both approaches. The instructional approach a program is based on can negatively or positively impact student mathematical learning and ultimately a school's overall mathematical performance. It is essential for educators to consider the design of the core mathematics program and its impact on student performance when designing an RTI system. All other decisions in the context of RTI are based on the core mathematics program. The more effective a core program is in progressing students to proficiency, the stronger the RTI system is as a whole.

Explicit instruction is, for the most part, teacher-led instructional lessons that focus specifically on the content (e.g., concepts, procedures, problem solving) that students are expected to learn. This is very different than student-centered instructional approaches wherein the teacher is more of a facilitator and students are responsible for constructing meaning on their own. Teachers utilizing methods of explicit instruction use clear, accurate, and multiple examples and demonstrations presented in small steps so students can clearly see what they are to learn. Along with the instructional demonstrations, students are provided ample opportunities to practice both with teacher support and independently to become proficient (i.e., master) with the content. It doesn't matter whether teachers are developing conceptual understanding, problem solving, and/or procedural knowledge; students who struggle require explicit methods of instruction.

Explicit teacher-directed instruction is much more than teacher demonstrations and is definitely not teacher lecture. There are six critical features of explicit instruction. First, each lesson starts with a daily review. This allows teachers to review content from previous lessons as well as revisit important preskills for the upcoming lesson. The daily review is followed by presentation of new content, which includes teacher-directed models and demonstrations with frequent questions and students actively involved in learning. Once students have started to acquire the new information, the teacher provides students with multiple opportunities for guided practice. Opportunities for guided practice can also occur through classwide peer tutoring. During guided practice, whether teacher guided or peer guided, students receive explicit feedback and corrective instruction for any mistakes. Teachers can also reteach if students are struggling. Once students have acquired the content, independent practice opportunities are provided to build proficiency and fluency. Finally, the systematic practice of providing weekly and monthly reviews is vital for students to maintain important mathematical concepts and skills. The level of explicitness during instruction can and should vary, but the importance of the explicitness for students who struggle or have learning disabilities cannot be overestimated as a research-validated instructional method (see Jayanthi, Gersten, & Baker, 2008; Kroesbergen & Van Luit, 2003; NMAP, 2008).

The Use of Concrete and Pictorial Representations

Several of the research studies reviewed employed the use of concrete manipulative objects and pictorial representations to demonstrate abstract concepts and procedures. It should be noted that students were not provided manipulative objects or pictorial representations to just figure out or play with, but rather they were combined with explicit instruction. It is the systematic and explicit use of the concrete and pictorial representations that have positive benefits for students (Witzel, 2005).

Teachers can supplement instruction with the use of concrete objects and pictorial representations, an instructional sequence that systematically progresses students through the concrete level of learning, then the pictorial representational level of learning, and then finally to the abstract level of learning, which has the strongest effect on student learning. One such effective approach to teaching mathematics is the Concrete to Representation to Abstract (CRA) sequence of instruction, which has been shown to improve students' understanding of computing fractions (Butler, Miller, Crehan, Babbitt, & Pierce, 2003; Jordan, Miller, & Mercer, 1999; Witzel & Riccomini, 2009), solving algebraic word problems for unknown quantities (Maccini & Hughes, 2000), and solving algebra transformation equations (Witzel, 2005; Witzel, Mercer, & Miller, 2003). CRA is discussed in more detail in Chapters 5 and 6.

Strategy Instruction for Problem Solving

Students with disabilities and those students who struggle in mathematics almost always demonstrate weaknesses in problem-solving ability. Students with poor problem-solving skills generally approach problems in an unorganized fashion, often just guess, and/or give up easily. The ability to solve problems is especially important as students get older and the math becomes more complex. The RTI studies that focused on problem-solving skills provided additional instruction in the form of a strategy (e.g., Hot Math, Schema-based Instruction) to help students approach word problems more systematically.

Students who struggle with learning are often not strategic in their approach to problem solving (Carnine, Silbert, Kame'enui, & Tarver, 2004). When you teach a student a strategy for problem solving, you are explicitly teaching an approach (step-by-step) used to solve a problem. The problem-solving approach can be a more general approach, such as RIDE (http://coe.jmu.edu/learningtoolbox): **R**ead the problem correctly, **I**dentify the relevant information, **D**etermine the operations and unit for expressing the answer, and **E**nter the correct numbers and calculate then check. A general or heuristic approach provides the student a strategy that can apply to a variety of problem-solving situations (Jayanthi et al., 2008).

A more specific problem-solving approach can be used such as a schema-based representational word problem–solving strategy (Jitendra, 2002; Jitendra & Hoff, 1996) where students are taught to recognize the word problem type and then use a corresponding diagram to solve the problem. Students will need some level of strategy instruction, either heuristic strategies or more specific strategies, to become strategic problem solvers. The effectiveness of strategy instruction to help students solve word problems is well documented, generally accepted as good practice for all students, and should become standard in all Tier 1 instruction. Chapter 8 will cover problem-solving strategies in more detail.

Focus on Basic Facts and Problem Solving

Almost all the studies focused on either basic facts or problem solving or both problem solving and basic facts. This is important due to the fact that the RTI studies reviewed targeted elementary students. The profile of an elementary student struggling in mathematics usually includes problems with automatic recall of basic facts as well as other areas of weakness. As students get older, the profile also includes basic computation and higher-order problem solving. A survey of 743 algebra teachers conducted by the NMAP (2008) reported that students need to be better prepared in basic math skills and not be so calculator dependent as well as receive more training on thinking skills. The NMAP (2008) also articulated critical benchmarks for specific mathematical skills involving proficiency with addition and subtraction by third grade and multiplication and division of whole numbers by fifth grade. The critical benchmarks also include fluency with fractions and with geometry and measurement (see Table 1.4). Students who do not have automatic recall of basic facts are likely to struggle with fractions and have little chance of success in algebra.

Clearly, automatic recall of basic facts is a major hurdle for many students and can interfere with students progressing to upper levels of mathematics courses. Instructional time devoted to automatic recall of basic facts should be included in the core math program but absolutely should be a focus in Tier 2 instruction for elementary and middle school students. Chapter 7 will discuss instruction to build proficiency with whole numbers and specific recommendations for automatic recall of basic facts.

Aligning Tier 1 and Tier 2 Instruction

Although careful alignment with Tier 1 and Tier 2 instruction did not occur across all the studies, the studies that did include this alignment had the best results for reducing the number of students who struggle in mathematics

Table 1.4 Recommended Benchmarks for Critical Foundations in Mathematics by Grade Level

Benchmark	Description
Fluency With Whole Numbers	By the end of Grade 3, students should be proficient with addition and subtraction of whole numbers.
	By the end of Grade 5, students should be proficient with multiplication and division of whole numbers.
Fluency With Fractions	By the end of Grade 4, students should be able to identify and represent fractions and decimals, and be able to compare them on a number line or with other common representations of fractions and decimals.
	By the end of Grade 5, students should be proficient with comparing fractions and decimals and common percent, and with the addition and subtraction of fractions and decimals.
	By the end of Grade 6, students should be proficient with multiplication and division of fractions and decimals.
	By the end of Grade 6, students should be proficient with all operations involving positive and negative integers.
	By the end of Grade 7, students should be proficient with all operations involving positive and negative fractions.
	By the end of Grade 7, students should be able to solve problems involving percent, ratio, and rate and extend this work to proportionality.
Geometry and Measurement	By the end of Grade 5, students should be able to solve problems involving perimeter and area of triangles and all quadrilaterals having at least one pair of parallel sides (e.g., trapezoids).
	By the end of Grade 6, students should be able to analyze the properties of two-dimensional shapes and solve problems involving perimeter and area, and analyze the properties of three-dimensional shapes and solve problems involving surface area and volume.
	By the end of Grade 7, students should be familiar with the relationship between similar triangles and the concept of the slope of a line.

Source: From the U.S. Department of Education, *Foundations for success: The final report of the National Mathematics Advisory Panel,* March 2008. Retrieved April 1, 2008, from http://www.ed.gov/about/bdscomm/list/ mathpanel/report/final-report.pdf.

at later grade levels. Obviously, the careful alignment of any additional supplemental instruction is critical for the ultimate success; however, this alignment can happen only if there is communication and collaboration between Tier 1 teachers and Tier 2 teachers. Although most educators recognize the importance of collaboration, communication, and planning, it isn't as common an occurrence as one would hope. A major component of an effective RTI model is careful alignment of supplemental instruction with the core math program and corresponding instruction.

Screening and Progress Monitoring to Target Deficit Areas

RTI models most often call for two forms of formative assessment: (1) universal screening and (2) progress monitoring and diagnostic assessments for struggling students. Universal screening is usually the first step in RTI and involves all students being assessed three to four times per year. The results of the universal screening are then used to identify students who are struggling with or are at risk for developing math disabilities. These students are then progress monitored more frequently. The frequency varies from once a month to as much as twice per week and depends on the ability and grade level of the student.

The main purpose of the progress-monitoring assessment is to evaluate program effectiveness as measured by student growth. If a student's trajectory is increasing at an appropriate rate, one can reasonably conclude that the instructional program is effective; if the trajectory is flat or decreasing, the instructional program is judged as not effective. These kinds of overall judgments are important and serve the purpose of program evaluation, but they do not necessarily identify specific areas of weakness to target for additional instruction.

The purpose of diagnostic assessments for struggling students is to identify specific deficit areas for each student. Once the specific areas are identified, teachers can better individualize instruction for their struggling students. Teachers can carefully examine the actual student work to better identify specific weaknesses to more efficiently provide instruction to struggling students (see Ashlock, 2006; Riccomini, 2005). This type of informed instructional decision making has two benefits: (1) Fewer students are referred for more in-depth evaluation because teachers can better address their weaknesses during instruction, and (2) those students that are ultimately referred for further evaluation are more likely to need special education services, thereby streamlining the entire process.

SUMMARY

This chapter has focused on the broad issues related to an effective RTI model applied to mathematics. RTI is a process that includes a series of procedures that must be carefully implemented and continually revised. As educators expand RTI procedures into mathematics, everyone involved must remember that the overall purpose is to provide better and more effective mathematics instruction to all students to increase the number of students proficient in mathematics and, therefore, to reduce the number of students requiring additional instruction and/or special education services. No matter what RTI model is selected, the most important aspect of the effectiveness is the additional instructional supports in Tiers 1 through 3. An effective Tier 1 core math program is the best way to ensure effective Tier 2 and Tier 3 instructional supports.

As research on RTI models in math continue to be conducted and disseminated, educators must use the results to guide their implementation. Currently, eight overarching principles for an effective RTI framework in mathematics have emerged from the research and include (1) increased instructional time and supports, (2) small-group instruction, (3) explicit methods of instruction, (4) the use of concrete and pictorial representations, (5) strategy instruction for problem solving, (6) focusing on basic facts and word problems, (7) aligning instruction from Tier 1 with Tier 2 to maximize the effectiveness, and (8) screening and progress monitoring to focus instruction on deficit areas. The remaining chapters will focus on specific instructional supports and interventions to improve the math performance of all students.

Emerging Themes From the Key Research on the Use of RTI Models in Math

1. Increased instructional time in addition to core mathematics program in Tier 1

2. Small-group instruction utilized in all tiers

3. Explicit methods of instruction provided to students on a regular basis in all tiers

4. Using concrete and pictorial representations to facilitate conceptual learning

5. Teaching students general and specific strategies for problem solving

6. Interventions that focus on basic facts as well as problem-solving skills

7. Careful alignment of instruction and content in Tier 1 and Tier 2

8. Screening and progress monitoring to better target deficit areas

Source: Adapted from Newman-Gonchar, R., Clarke, B., & Gersten, R. (2009). *A summary of nine key studies: Multitier intervention and response to interventions for students struggling in mathematics.* Portsmouth, NH: RMC Research Corporation, Center on Instruction. Retrieved February 1, 2009, from www.centeroninstruction.com.

The RTI Process for Math 2

Getting Started

High-quality research should play a central role in any effort to improve mathematics learning.

—*Adding It Up: Helping Children Learn Mathematics*
(National Research Council [NRC], 2001), p. 26

As educators expand RTI into the content area of mathematics, many aspects used in reading apply, but some differences also exist. Odds are great that if your school is considering an RTI model in mathematics, a model in reading already exists. Many of the overall principles will be the same across content area; however, the process of implementation of an RTI model is slightly different and more involved than the six guiding principles discussed in Chapter 1.

The purpose of this chapter is to provide a general guide to getting an RTI model started in mathematics that can be slightly modified to fit your school's specific needs, resources, teachers, and students. It is our hope that this chapter provides general guidance on forming the school-level RTI Team, a description of the essential components to consider when designing and implementing an RTI model in math, common RTI approaches, assessment issues, and the importance of the core mathematics program and instruction.

SELECTION OF THE RTI TEAM MEMBERS

RTI is a team effort; however, it is difficult to stipulate exactly who should be on the RTI team because each school is composed of staff with differing areas of expertise and experience. To incorporate an RTI program successfully, the members of an RTI team must be carefully selected and include a variety of individuals with specific capabilities and responsibilities. The process and procedures involved in an efficient RTI system requires collaboration among the administration, teachers—both general and special education—and specialists within the school. To help schools select a school-level RTI team, it may be helpful to first discuss the responsibilities of the RTI team.

In general, the overall purpose of the RTI team is to examine the efficacy of a school's assessment and instructional system with the intent of systematically refining the system to be more effective. Specifically, the members of the RTI team are responsible for at least the following seven actions: (1) assessment of the instructional environment, (2) instructional problem solving, (3) determination of the appropriate research-based interventions, (4) determining who will implement intervention and where it is implemented, (5) monitoring and evaluating treatment fidelity, (6) continuous data review and evaluation of students' response to the interventions, and (7) maximizing available resources considered necessary for successful implementation. Additionally, members of the RTI may be required to provide coaching for teachers learning to implement new and unfamiliar instructional strategies. The coaching of teachers as they begin using the determined research-based instructional strategies is a critical step to the fidelity of interventions and probably the one that is most often overlooked. High-quality professional development and follow-up support will certainly allow for a more even implementation.

Assuming the RTI team will be responsible for the above described actions, at the very least the members should consist of the principal, curricular coordinator (if available), general education teacher, special education teacher, school psychologists, and various other school specialists that may be available. Title I staff play an important role in providing supplemental services to students, and therefore, it may be beneficial to have these staff as members of the RTI team.

Specifically to the area of mathematics, if a math specialist is not available in your school, it is important for a member of the RTI team to have content expertise in mathematics. It may even be advisable to include a mathematics teacher from the secondary level to provide input into what content Tier 2 should prioritize and focus on. The RTI team involves a collaborative effort among school staff with specialized expertise and experiences that when combined are a powerful change agent in the continued improvement of instructional programs and interventions for all students.

BELIEF SYSTEM

The belief system of teachers and professionals in the school can have a positive and/or negative impact on the effectiveness of the RTI model. All involved educators must take responsibility and ownership in the RTI process. Students should not be viewed as special education students, Title 1 students, or general education students, but rather as everyone's students. Three general beliefs about teaching and learning should be established in the planning stages of RTI and include the following: (1) All educators want children to learn, (2) all parents want children to learn, and (3) all children want to learn.

These three general beliefs about learning are vital to a successful RTI model in any content area; however, specific to RTI in mathematics, teachers must have four common core beliefs: (1) All students can be mathematically proficient; (2) all students need a high-quality mathematics program; (3) effective mathematics instructional programs must teach

> "All students can and should be mathematically proficient in Grades pre-K through 8."
>
> —*Adding It Up: Helping Children Learn Mathematics (NRC, 2001), p. 10*

conceptual understanding, computational fluency, factual knowledge, and problem-solving skills; and (4) effective instruction matters and significantly impacts student learning and achievement in mathematics. A brief discussion of each core belief is presented below.

Core Belief #1: All Students Can Be Mathematically Proficient

Mathematics difficulties, unlike reading problems, are sometimes overlooked or attributed to the idea that not everyone can be proficient in mathematics. Even parents will often excuse their own children's problems in math as "not that important" or justify problems by saying, "I wasn't very good in math when I was a kid." This mind-set toward learning math is very different than that toward reading. It should be an accepted belief that all students can be mathematically proficient starting in pre-K and continuing through eighth grade and

> "All students need access to a high-quality mathematics program."
>
> —*National Mathematics Advisory Panel, 2008*

hopefully all the way through high school (National Mathematics Advisory Panel [NMAP], 2008; National Research Council, 2001). If teachers, parents, and students lack the fundamental goal that all students can become proficient in mathematics at least through Grade 8, an effective RTI model is likely to be less effective. The goal of proficiency for all students is directly related to the next two core beliefs.

Core Belief #2: All Students Need a High-Quality Mathematics Program

For all students to reach mathematical proficiency, students need a high-quality mathematics program designed to prepare them for more advanced mathematics courses as well as for postsecondary school and/or various careers. The emphasis on high-quality mathematics programs is sometimes pursued by states enacting higher standards of learning. This is important, but it does not guarantee a high-quality mathematics program. Standards are the goals for learning; an effective mathematics program must have high standards but also include effective delivery (i.e., instruction) of the standards.

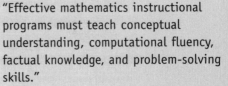

> "Effective mathematics instructional programs must teach conceptual understanding, computational fluency, factual knowledge, and problem-solving skills."
>
> —*National Mathematics Advisory Panel, 2008*

We will not go into detail regarding state standards because every state has their own set of standards, but rather we will discuss later in this chapter the importance of core mathematics programs.

Core Belief #3: Effective Mathematics Programs Must Teach Conceptual Understanding, Computational Fluency, Factual Knowledge, and Problem-Solving Skills

The next core belief regarding "what should be taught" has received a great deal of attention and often heated debate. The NMAP (2008) recommends that effective core mathematics programs build conceptual understanding, procedural knowledge, factual fluency, and problem-solving skills. Bottom line: students who are mathematically proficient are able to solve problems through the application of a variety of strategies while applying mathematical concepts and procedures and are both accurate and fluent in the process. Mathematical programs must reflect this belief by addressing each area through content instruction, learning activities, and appropriate and sufficient opportunities to practice.

Everyone involved in the mathematics instructional program must recognize the importance of conceptual understanding, procedural knowledge, factual fluency, and problem solving. Each area must receive instructional attention by teachers if students are to become mathematically proficient, especially in Tier 1. It may help to discuss the meaning of "mathematically proficient" with those teachers teaching and supporting math. The NMAP (2008) provides the following definition:

> Proficiency means that students should understand key concepts; achieve automaticity as appropriate (e.g., with addition and related subtraction facts); develop flexible, accurate, and automatic execution of the standard algorithms; and use these competencies to solve problems.

Similarly, the National Research Council (2001) explains proficiency in mathematics with five interconnected strands: (1) understanding mathematics, (2) computing fluently, (3) applying concepts to solve problems, (4) reasoning logically, and (5) engaging with mathematics. Within each strand numerous concepts, procedures, algorithms, and computations are important for students to learn, understand, and connect. Proficiency in mathematics depends on a continuous growth and blend of intricate combinations of critical component skills (e.g., concepts, procedures, algorithms, computation). If teachers do not recognize the importance of each of these areas during instruction, a school's RTI model will be less effective.

> "All-encompassing recommendations that instruction should be entirely 'student centered' or 'teacher directed' are not supported by research."
>
> —*National Mathematics Advisory Panel, 2008*

Along with these definitions, teachers must consider their state's definition of mathematical proficiency as well. Careful review and analysis of state standards, commercially available core mathematics curricula, and interventions as well as other resources must be done with precision. Regardless of the definition of proficiency, students must have a working knowledge of concepts, procedures, facts, and problem solving. Deciding what to teach is a vital aspect that must be established and agreed upon, because if teachers don't value certain aspects of math (e.g., automatic recall of basic facts, conceptual understanding), they are likely to not focus instruction in the area. Once your school has established the "what to teach" core belief, the next area to establish is the "how you teach."

Core Belief #4: Effective Instruction Matters and Significantly Impacts Student Learning

The field of mathematics education has what can be described as the equivalent of the "reading wars," which have existed since the 1980s and still exist today to some extent. The reading field argued, debated, criticized, and demonized two approaches to teaching literacy: (1) "whole language" and (2) "phonics based." The debate went on for years despite the overwhelming research evidence supporting the importance of phonics. Unfortunately, the field of mathematics' research base is not as robust or developed as the field of reading's research base, but it does have a sufficient enough research base to begin to make important recommendations and conclusions about "how to teach math." What is most important for teachers to recognize is that the instruction they deliver has a direct impact on student learning.

The instructional debate in mathematics revolves around two approaches to teaching mathematics: (1) student centered or (2) teacher directed. A student-centered approach is generally associated with inquiry learning and/or discovery learning with the teacher taking on the role of a facilitator helping or guiding students to construct meaning. A teacher-directed approach is generally associated with direct instruction, explicit instruction, and/or teacher-led instruction. The responsibility is placed on the teacher to directly teach students important information. It is our experience that many general education teachers (Tier 1) are encouraged to choose a student-centered style of teaching. However, special education teachers and those working with struggling students are encouraged to select a teacher-directed approach. Our experiences as well as research indicate there is an appropriate time for both student- and teacher-centered approaches during math class.

It is not our intent to spark this debate but rather to recognize that the instructional approach can impact student learning, and this is especially true for students who are struggling. In an effort to provide insight on the two instructional approaches, the NMAP (2008) reviewed high-quality research involving the two teaching approaches and concluded the following:

1. All-encompassing recommendations that instruction should be entirely "student centered" or "teacher directed" are not supported by research.
   a. If such recommendations exist, they should be rescinded.
   b. If they are being considered, they should be avoided.
   c. High-quality research does not support the exclusive use of either approach.

2. Students with learning disabilities and other students with learning problems (e.g., low achievers, at risk, difficulties in mathematics) should receive on a regular basis some explicit systematic instruction that includes the following:

    a. Clear problem-solving models
    b. Carefully orchestrated examples and sequences of examples
    c. Concrete objects to understand abstract representations and notation
    d. Opportunities for students to participate and hear teachers thinking aloud

These two findings have enormous implications for setting up an effective RTI model in mathematics. Especially relevant to RTI is the recommendation that students with learning disabilities and those who are struggling have regular access to systematic and explicit instruction (i.e., teacher directed), and failing to do so may be a major barrier to implementation of an effective RTI model in mathematics.

Pragmatically, what this means is Tier 1 teachers (i.e., the general education math teacher using the core mathematics curriculum) must provide some level of explicit instruction before students move into the next tier. If the general education teacher does not share this belief or instructional pedagogy, students who struggle will not be effectively taught by the general education teacher before moving into Tier 2 instructional supports. This will result in a less effective RTI model and ultimately more students requiring additional instructional supports. Therefore, this is the main reason why this book is being written, and we will focus mostly on the application of explicit instruction to the teaching of mathematics concepts.

The NMAP's (2008) recommendations should not be taken in isolation, but rather with other available findings from research. At the end of Chapter 1, we reviewed nine key research studies involving RTI in math; the conclusions are similar to the NMAP recommendation regarding access to explicit instruction. The type of instruction provided to students impacts learning either positively or negatively. This belief must be recognized and addressed. If the general education mathematics curriculum and instruction (Tier 1) is completely student centered, your school's RTI model has a fatal flaw and will not be effective.

It is not our intent to sound alarms, but unwillingness by general education mathematics teachers to provide some level of systematic and explicit instruction (i.e., teacher directed) in Tier 1 will negatively impact an RTI model. If this is the case, time must be devoted to discuss and resolve this instructional approach issue or at least come to an agreement that some students need regular access to explicit instruction and set up a plan to provide students this type of instruction in Tier 1; a balance is needed. The decision on how to teach should be guided by high-quality research and based on students' performance and instructional needs; decisions of how to teach should not be based solely on teachers' philosophies.

> Decisions regarding how to teach (student centered or teacher directed) should be guided by high-quality research and based on student performance and instructional needs, not solely on teachers' philosophies.

To conclude the discussion on core RTI beliefs, we provide a Core Belief System Rating Checklist (see Table 2.1). The checklist will help serve as a self-analysis on teachers' views and core beliefs about teaching and learning mathematics and help to set a positive tone for the mathematics program. It is recommended that at least 80%–90% of teachers involved in the RTI process recognize and accept all four core RTI beliefs discussed here; if they do not, a school leadership team should be formed to explore areas in which teachers have diverging beliefs about teaching and learning mathematics to help establish common ground from which to build upon.

Unfortunately, our experience working in schools over the past 10 years taught us that beliefs about teaching and learning are often deep-rooted and very different from teacher to teacher, and they are not always shared or productive even in the face of plummeting student mathematical performance. This is an important first step to implementing RTI in mathematics and should not be overlooked or taken for granted.

Table 2.1 Core Belief System Rating Checklist		
Core Belief	*Agree*	*Disagree*
1. All students can be mathematically proficient.		
2. All students need a high-quality mathematics program.		
3. Effective mathematics instructional programs must teach conceptual understanding, computational fluency, factual knowledge, and problem-solving skills.		
4. Effective instruction matters and significantly impacts student learning and achievement in mathematics.		
5. General education teachers will use a balance of "student-centered" and "teacher-directed" instruction in the core mathematics program when appropriate before moving students into Tier 2.		

Note: This checklist can act as a starting point, and modifications and additions to the core beliefs specific to your school and state standards are encouraged. It is an important first step to get everyone on the same page. Additionally, other similar checklists are available and can be used.

COMMON MODELS OF IMPLEMENTATION

Once your school has established its belief system, selection of your approach to implementation is also very important to the success of your RTI model. For the past 5 years, educators have spent considerable effort and time developing and refining their specific procedures used to implement RTI. Although the

> A specific RTI approach will not guarantee success, but rather the quality and intensity of the instruction and assessment procedures will impact effectiveness.

specific procedures vary across schools, there are two basic approaches used: (1) standardized protocol model and (2) problem-solving model. A third approach that combines components of both the standardized protocol model and problem-solving model is emerging.

Standardized Protocol Model

A standardized protocol model is exactly what the name implies: standard. Within a standardized protocol model, the procedures for implementation are the same and apply to all students. A school using a standardized protocol model will use the same intervention to provide additional instruction for students failing to make adequate progress in the core mathematics program. Each tier of instructional supports looks the same for all students (see Figure 2.1).

For example, the Smithfield school district has decided that all second-grade students struggling in mathematics will receive an additional 15 minutes of small-group instruction five times a week focusing on the basic number operations in Tier 1; this is in addition to the 60 minutes spent on the core mathematics program every day. After 5 additional weeks of progress monitoring of the additional instruction, all students who continue to struggle will move into Tier 2 instruction. The RTI team has designated that any student who is below the 40th percentile will receive Tier 2 instruction.

The Tier 2 intervention will consist of small-group instruction (e.g., 5–10 students) implemented by a highly qualified teacher with special training in explicit instruction and differentiated instructional strategies. The focus of the Tier 2 intervention for all students will be 5 minutes devoted to fact fluency and automaticity practice, 20 minutes devoted to problem-solving strategies, and 10 minutes devoted to essential vocabulary. The Tier 2 intervention will last approximately 10–12 weeks with progress monitoring occurring once a week.

At the end of the Tier 2 intervention, three decisions can be made by the RTI team: (1) Student has met goal and returns to Tier 1 instruction only, (2) student made adequate progress and is on track to meet end-of-year benchmarks and will continue with Tier 1 and Tier 2 instructional supports, and (3) student made inadequate or no progress and will move into Tier 3. At this point, a need for further diagnostics testing may exist to determine specific deficit areas to help prescribe more targeted and intensive instruction as well as eligibility decisions.

Problem-Solving Model

A problem-solving model attempts to address struggling students on an individual basis. Unlike a standardized protocol model where all students receive the same intervention, in a problem-solving model, interventions are matched to individual student strengths and weaknesses (see Figure 2.2). This is generally accomplished through a team approach where the team carefully

Figure 2.1 Standard Protocol Model Flowchart

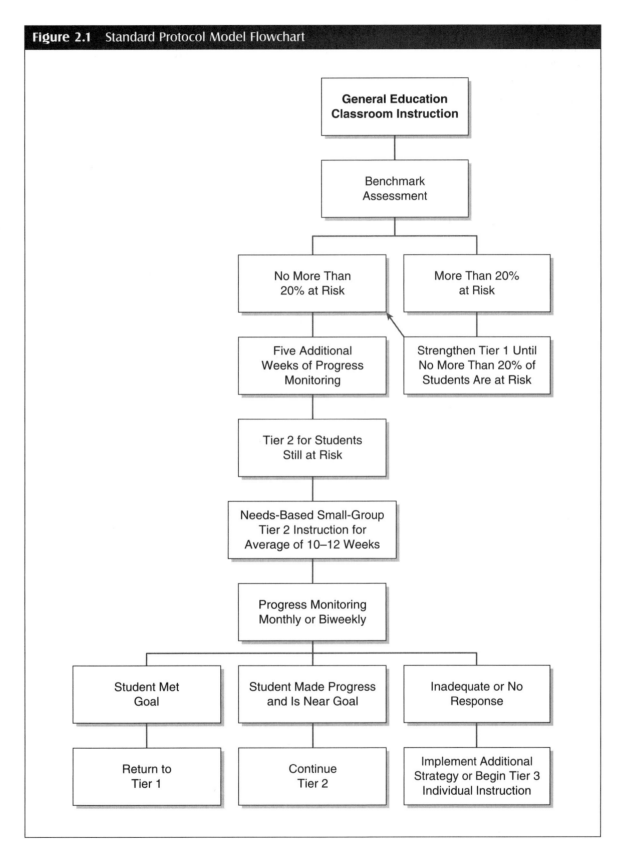

Source: Shores, C., & Chester, K. (2009). *Using RTI for school improvement: Raising every student's achievement scores.* Thousand Oaks, CA: Corwin. ISBN 978-1-4129-6641-2

Figure 2.2 Problem-Solving RTI Model Flowchart

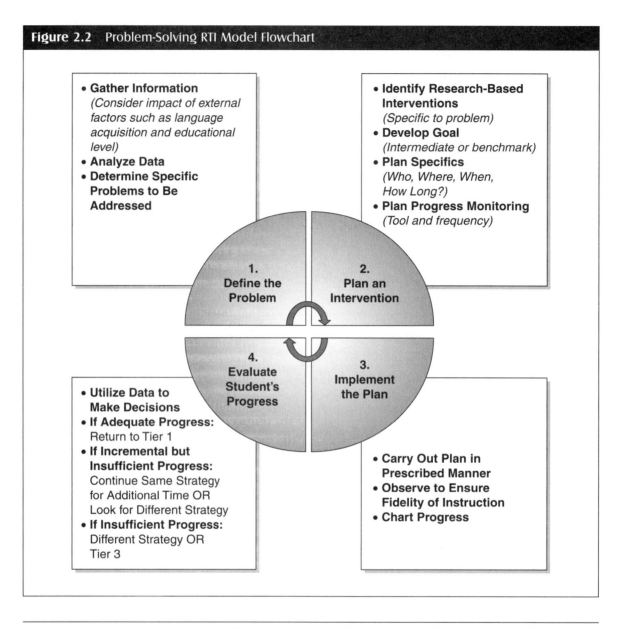

Source: Shores, C., & Chester, K. (2009). *Using RTI for school improvement: Raising every student's achievement scores.* Thousand Oaks, CA: Corwin. ISBN 978-1-4129-6641-2

examines student performance data and identifies the weakest areas and then designs a plan for additional individualized instructional support.

For example, two students in Ms. Smith's math class are not making progress and she refers them to the school's RTI team. The RTI team gathers all available information relating to each student's math performance. After analyzing the data, the team determines that one student is experiencing problems with basic computation and the other student is struggling with word problems in part due to poor reading and underdeveloped mathematical vocabulary. The RTI team meets with the math teacher, Ms. Smith, to develop an intervention that she will implement in addition to the core mathematics program. The team develops a plan for Ms. Smith to provide 15 minutes of supplemental math instruction three times a week for the next 6 weeks for both students. The student experiencing difficulties with basic computation will receive instruction focusing on basic fact fluency and automaticity, while the other student will be taught a strategy to solve world problems and receive vocabulary instruction on essential math terms. Each student has a specific goal based on their current levels of performance and appropriate growth rates. Ms. Smith will progress monitor every other week for 6 weeks and display the data graphically.

At the end of the 6-week intervention in Tier 1, student progress-monitoring data will be analyzed by the RTI team. The team determines that the student who had been struggling with word problems has made adequate progress with the strategy instruction and no longer needs the additional instructional support; the student has generalized the strategy across math problems. The student will be progress monitored once a month for the next 4 months to determine progress and make sure the student doesn't start struggling again. The student who is experiencing problems with basic number operations has made very little progress and will move into Tier 2 instructional supports.

Tier 2 instructional supports involve 30 minutes every day for the next 6 weeks and will focus on automatic recall of basic facts as well as some additional practice opportunities on computation procedures. The Tier 2 intervention is teacher directed and occurs in small homogenous groups. The student will continue to receive the 15 minutes of additional instruction in Ms. Smith's classroom while also receiving 30 minutes of instruction in Tier 2. Progress monitoring is now increased to once a week over the duration of the Tier 2 intervention and is used by the RTI team's decision-making process to determine if additional and/or different Tier 2 and Tier 3 instructional supports as well as possible eligibility determination are required.

Hybrid Model Approach

The new hybrid vehicles take advantage of technology from both traditional gasoline-powered automobiles and battery-powered vehicles to run more efficiently. Similarly, a hybrid approach to RTI maximizes the advantages of both the standardized protocol and the problem-solving approach to improving instruction. For example, in mathematics, there are certain content areas in which many students will require additional instruction and opportunities to practice before becoming proficient, such as problem solving and automatic recall of basic facts. Using components of the standardized protocol, the first areas targeted for additional instruction are problem solving and automatic recall of basic facts. The more these areas are addressed in the Tier 1 classroom instruction, the lower the number of students requiring additional supports for these areas in Tier 2. Sometimes this involves two "core" mathematics programs. Now, one is not really a true "core" mathematics program, but rather a supplemental program that *all* students receive in the context of the regular education mathematics classroom—Tier 2. This second core is targeting specific areas of weakness as identified by the RTI team using state assessments, district benchmarks, universal screening data, and teacher experiences.

Following the set period of time for additional instruction and practice targeting problem solving and automatic recall of basic facts, progress-monitoring data are used to identify students who did not make adequate progress. Using components of a problem-solving approach, an RTI team now examines all available assessment data (e.g., progress monitoring, district or state benchmarks, informal teacher tests, etc.) of the students who are still struggling. Based on the RTI team's analysis, an individualized instructional intervention is designed and implemented. By blending components of both approaches, educators are better able to maximize resources and student learning. This also allows for a careful alignment of Tier 1 and Tier 2 instructional supports. In other words, Tier 2 instruction is directly supporting Tier 1 instruction. The RTI team continues to monitor student progress and make appropriate decisions similar to the three decisions made in the standardized protocol model.

Students who are still not making adequate progress are moved into Tier 3 instructional supports. In a hybrid model, these students have received multiple levels of supports in Tiers 1 and 2 and are still not making adequate progress. Tier 3 instruction could involve a totally new core mathematics program with the purpose of still delivering standards-based instruction, but in a much more intensive and systematic and explicit approach. As students in Tier 3 progress through the instructional plan, documentation of progress-monitoring data and instructional supports from all the tiers is especially important because of possible eligibility decisions that will have to be made.

Although we have presented simplified descriptions of three approaches to RTI, the most important aspect of the models is the plan to provide additional instruction and supports for students identified as struggling. The information presented above is general and should be carefully considered within the context of the specific needs, resources, and experience of your school. There is no "one way" or "right way" to implement RTI (as of yet); however, improved student learning is the key to deciding if your approach is effective. Additionally, the specific model, whether it be problem solving, standard protocol, or hybrid, will not necessarily dictate success, but rather the quality and intensity of the instruction and assessment procedures will ultimately have the most impact on the effectiveness.

ASSESSMENT

An important aspect in any RTI model is assessment. Assessment serves at least three main purposes for teachers in an RTI model: (1) It provides information from which to start planning current performance, (2) it recognizes students in need of further instruction, and (3) it provides evidence of student progress and program effectiveness. The assessment approach most associated with an RTI system is curriculum-based measurement.

Curriculum-based measurement (CBM) refers to an approach for measuring students' rate of learning in reading, mathematics, writing, and spelling using a series of technically adequate short parallel-form assessments repeated frequently across the year. CBM comprises a number of different but related evidenced-based assessment tools used by teachers to make instructional decisions to improve achievement. The various assessment tools associated with CBM are based on more than 30 years of educational research completed with diverse learners and across multiple content areas. Overwhelmingly, positive evidence exists when teachers use CBM data to make informed instructional decisions when planning current and future instruction (Stecker, Fuchs, & Fuchs, 2005). In addition to enhancing the academic performance of low-performing as well as average- and above-average-achieving students, students with disabilities also benefit from teachers' use of CBM data.

Much has been written and researched regarding CBM and assessment procedures utilized within an RTI model; therefore, we are providing a general overview of three assessment types inherent in any RTI approach: (1) universal screening, (2) progress monitoring, and (3) diagnostic evaluation. Additionally, a table of frequently asked questions about CBM math and a resource list on RTI assessments are contained in Table 2.2 and Table 2.3, respectively. For more detailed information regarding assessments within an RTI model, see the publication *RTI: Assessment Essentials for Struggling Learners* by John Hoover (2009).

Table 2.2 Frequently Asked Questions About CBM and Math	
Question	*Answer*
Do teachers generally administer math CBM sheets one-on-one with each student or to a group?	It depends on the teacher and the purpose. When screening a whole class, it makes more sense to administer to the entire group. When doing weekly progress monitoring, you might do it individually or with a small group of two to three students.
My student has improved his/her math performance as I have monitored progress, but she/he is not receiving any instruction in math. Could assessing using CBM alone be making a difference?	The extra 2 minutes of practice that she/he is getting per week is probably not enough to show improvement. She/he may be practicing elsewhere or receiving additional instruction.
I have only 20 math CBM sheets, but I need to progress monitor for 35 weeks. Is it OK to use the same sheets again?	Yes. Once you have used all 20, start using them again. The student probably doesn't remember specific items she/he did 20 weeks ago. This also means that you should not use the math sheets as homework or additional practice if you want to use them again.
Should I tell my students that they get credit for each part of the computation problems rather than just correct/incorrect for the problem?	No, because it's the answer that is most important. If a student is concentrating on the intermediate stages even though he/she can calculate a complex problem in his/her head,

Table 2.2 (Continued)	
Question	*Answer*
	she/he may show work she/he doesn't need to. This would slow him/her down by adding unnecessary steps. You want to get an authentic measure of student performance.
Because math CBM measures fluency, skipping time-consuming problems might be a calculated choice so that the student can move on to problems that can be solved more quickly. Does not answering specific questions really indicate a gap in skills, or could it be a logical strategy?	More complex problems have more correct digits associated with them, so it's a flawed strategy anyway. If a student is skipping certain problem types, you should administer a single-skill sheet to determine if she/he can't or won't perform that type of problem. Sometimes the solution is as simple as asking the student, "Why did you skip these problems?" If the answer is "So I could finish more of the easier ones," you should remind the student to attempt every problem and have the student complete another sheet.
Can I use benchmark scores on math CBM to put students in instructional groups?	Yes, if you have students with similar instructional needs. These groups should be flexible and students should be evaluated and regrouped every 6–8 weeks.
Not everyone in my class is on the same instructional level. Should I still give all the same math CBM sheets?	All students should be screened/ benchmarked on their grade level, but they should be progress monitored on their instructional level, especially if they are receiving instruction on that level. The best way to handle this is to give both the grade-level and instructional-level math sheets each week so that you have an indication of how students are doing given the instruction they are receiving and how well it is transferring to the more difficult problems.
What should I do with the scored CBM math sheets?	This information can be kept in a portfolio along with graphed data to demonstrate progress over the year.

Source: Hosp, M. K., Hosp, J. L., & Howell, K. W. (2007). *The ABCs of CBM: A practical guide to curriculum-based measurement.* New York: Guilford Press.

Table 2.3   Assessments Within Three-Tiered Instruction

Tier	Assessment	Expected Outcome	Evidence of Struggling Learner
Core	Universal Screening	Learner successfully meets curricular benchmarks; makes satisfactory rate of progress.	Scores are below expected curricular benchmark standards as indicated by universal screening results; learner fails to make satisfactory rate of progress.
Supplemental	Progress Monitoring	Supplemental supports assist learner to meet curricular objectives/standards found in Core instruction; student makes satisfactory rate of progress.	Supplemental supports do not assist learner to meet Core objectives/standards—minimum of two rounds of Tier 2 supplemental supports; learner fails to make adequate rate of progress as evidenced by more frequent progress monitoring.
Intensive	Progress Monitoring; Diagnostic	Intensive interventions assist learner to make satisfactory rate of progress and/or achieve minimum acceptable level of progress toward achieving curricular benchmarks/objectives.	Student continues to make inadequate progress toward curricular benchmarks/objectives after extended period of time receiving intensive instruction designed to meet special needs; special education diagnostic assessment further clarifies special needs along with highly frequent progress monitoring.

Source: Hoover, J. H. (2009). *RTI: Assessment essentials for struggling learners.* Thousand Oaks, CA: Corwin. ISBN: 978-1-4129-6954-3

Universal Screening

The use of a universal screening assessment is a critical first step in an RTI system. The purpose of the universal screening is twofold: (1) to identify students who are at risk or already struggling in mathematics so that teachers can immediately begin more intensive instruction, and (2) to follow (i.e., monitor) students who were not struggling initially but might begin to struggle later in the year. It is important that *all* students participate whether they initially struggle or not. We would like to emphasize that the purpose of universal screening assessments is *not* to identify more students for special education services.

Generally, the universal screening assessments are given three to four times per year with assessment times ranging from 5 to 20 minutes depending on grade level and content (Gersten et al., 2009). As schools begin the process of selecting a universal screening measure and planning the data collection process, several key ideas warrant careful consideration by RTI teams.

When selecting a universal screening measure, Gersten and colleagues recommend that the RTI teams examine three key points of the measure: (1) predictive validity, (2) reliability, and (3) efficiency of administration. The predictive validity of a measure indicates how well a score forecasts the student's later math performance. Clearly, a higher predictive validity allows schools much more confidence in decisions based on the universal screening measure. The universal screening measure selected should have a predictive validity coefficient of at least .60 (Gersten et al., 2009). An assessment's reliability is an indication of the consistency and accuracy of the measure; a reliability coefficient of at least .80 is recommended (Gersten et al., 2009). One of the most important characteristics of a universal screening measure to consider is the length of administration.

Because universal screening is completed on the entire school population, it is imperative that the measure is administered in a short period of time. Gersten and colleagues recommend no more than 20 minutes, but there are reliable and valid measures available that can be administered in as little as 5 minutes. The length of administration is important because longer measures will require more time to administer and thereby use valuable instructional time. Following the selection of the screening measure, collection of data, and subsequent analysis of the results, students who are struggling or at risk are then progress monitored.

Progress Monitoring

Progress monitoring is the frequent assessment of struggling students for the purpose of evaluating their learning in relationship to end-of-year goals. Additionally, within an RTI system, progress monitoring is used to evaluate the effectiveness of an intervention. Similar considerations described above for universal screening should also be considered for the selection of progress-monitoring measures.

Generally, the assessments are brief (5–10 minutes) and are given at least once a month and as frequently as twice a week. Depending on the grade level of the progress-monitoring measure, most measures target number sense (e.g., counting, quantity comparisons), computation of whole numbers, and problem solving. Progress-monitoring assessments are almost always timed and are a measure of fluency. Unlike progress-monitoring assessments in reading that require one-to-one administration, progress-monitoring mathematics assessments can be given to an entire class and scored at a later date. This aspect of progress monitoring in mathematics allows for easier administration and limits the instructional disruptions.

There are many different commercial progress-monitoring assessments available currently, and probably many more will be available by the time this book is published, so we will not attempt to describe in detail available assessments; however, there are some general principles of progress-monitoring assessments. The administration, directions, and scoring are standard for each assessment and consistent across the year. Teachers should not under any circumstances change the administration procedures, directions, and/or the time allocations of the assessments unless it is an allowable change approved by the publisher of the assessment. This is critical because the results are compared to benchmarks and/or norms that were collected under the same conditions of administration, directions, and time allocations; changing any of the standard procedures can nullify the relationship to the norms/benchmarks used to evaluate student progress. For example, we often hear teachers state that a student doesn't work well under timing conditions and they want to give the student additional time during the first several assessments and then reduce the time as the student progresses through the year. This is an incorrect approach and defeats the purpose of progress monitoring. The purpose of progress monitoring is to measure student progress across the year. For the data to be reliable and valid, the students must take the assessments under the same conditions (i.e., administration, directions, and time allocations) each and every time in order to make accurate decisions.

Since progress-monitoring assessments are evaluating student learning across the year, the results can be used to evaluate the effectiveness of the instructional program. If students are learning, we can conclude with relative confidence that the instructional program is effective for the student. If the student is not demonstrating increased learning, we then can conclude that the instructional program is not effective for the student and requires instructional changes. This is an important aspect for an RTI model in mathematics and is directly connected to progress-monitoring data.

Diagnostic Assessments

The purpose of diagnostic assessments is to provide more detailed information regarding specific strengths and weaknesses. As students are progress monitored and provided instructional supports based on those results, diagnostic assessments may be needed at some point to determine specific areas to target. Generally, progress-monitoring measures and universal screening are broader measures and are not intended for diagnostic purposes. Although it is possible to ascertain specific areas of weakness through analysis of progress-monitoring measures, diagnostic assessments are appropriate for students who are not showing any progress. As schools begin to use RTI procedures for identification and entitlement purposes, diagnostic assessments should be part of the information used in these high-stakes decisions; progress-monitoring data and universal screening assessments can provide important information but should not be the only information used for eligibility decisions.

National Center on Student Progress Monitoring

At the time of this publication, the National Center on Student Progress Monitoring (www.studentprogress.org) had reviewed five measures identified for universal screening and progress monitoring: (1) Accelerated Math and

Reader, (2) AIMSweb, (3) Monitoring Basic Skills Progress, (4) PA Series, and (5) Yearly Progress Pro. It is important to note that the list is not necessarily comprehensive, and the center neither endorses nor recommends any one particular assessment.

The center's staff conducted a comprehensive review of several assessments in relationship to foundational psychometric standards including reliability and validity, and five standards of progress monitoring: (1) providing alternate forms, (2) being sensitive to student improvement, (3) attaining adult yearly progress (AYP) benchmarks, (4) improving student learning or teacher planning, and (5) specifying rates of improvement. The results of the review can be found under the <Tools> tab on the center's home page. By clicking on the assessment's name <Math>, additional information about each assessment is provided and includes (a) cost; (b) technology, human resources, and accommodations for special needs; (c) service and support; (d) purpose and other implementation information; and (e) usage and reporting. The results are presented in an easy-to-read table format, and a black dot in any column indicates that that particular aspect was demonstrated as sufficient.

For up-to-date information related to all aspects of progress monitoring and RTI assessment procedures, visit the National Center on Student Progress Monitoring at www.studentprogress.org and the National Center on Response to Intervention at www.rti4success.org. When selecting an assessment for RTI math, the National Center on Student Progress Monitoring contains information that can assist in the selection process and should be your first stop.

Assessments are a necessary aspect of an RTI model, but not necessarily sufficient for improving student learning. Teachers must use the data systematically and regularly to make appropriate instructional decisions. The process by which teachers are able to routinely integrate progress-monitoring data analysis and instructional decisions is the most essential and often most challenging aspect of an effective RTI model.

Math Progress-Monitoring Resources

The following resources contain information and products relating the universal screening and progress monitoring of mathematics performance:

AIMSweb Progress Monitoring and RTI System: www.aimsweb.com

AIMSweb is a progress-monitoring system based on direct, frequent, and continuous student assessment in the areas of reading, mathematics, spelling, and written expression. The results are reported to students, parents, teachers, and administrators via a Web-based data management and reporting system to determine response to intervention.

AplusMath: www.aplusmath.com

AplusMath is a free Web site developed to help students improve their math skills interactively. It has premade single-skill sheets on a wide range of math skills from addition to fractions to basic algebra. A worksheet generator is also available to make mixed-skills math sheets.

Edcheckup: www.edcheckup.com

Edcheckup™ offers a progress-monitoring system for students in Grades K–8 that evaluates student performance and measures student progress toward goals in reading, writing, and math. These generic assessments, which are independent from any particular curriculum, may also be used to evaluate the effectiveness of instruction through the graphing of student data.

EdProgress: www.edprogress.com

EdProgress focuses on assessment, large-scale testing and accountability, and systemic reform. With research-proven training materials, measurement tools, reporting systems, and teacher training interventions, EdProgress helps teachers become more focused on teaching and learning for all students.

easyCBM: http://easycbm.com

easyCBM is a Web site dedicated to progress monitoring in the areas of reading and mathematics in Grades K–8. The Web site offers data management, measures, report generating, password-protected accounts, and training on administration and scoring of measures used by easyCBM.

Intervention Central: www.interventioncentral.org

Intervention Central offers free tools and resources to help school staff and parents to promote positive classroom behaviors and foster effective learning for all children and youth. Visit to check out newly posted academic and behavioral intervention strategies, download publications on effective teaching practices, and use tools that streamline classroom assessment and intervention in the areas of reading, mathematics, spelling, and written expression.

Monitoring Basic Skills Progress: www.proedinc.com

The Monitoring Basic Skills Progress (MBSP) Blackline Masters are a research-based standardized set of measurement and evaluation procedures. They provide a method to focus intensively on the math progress of individual students who have identified learning problems and to evaluate formatively and improve those students' programs.

National Center on Student Progress Monitoring: www.studentprogress.org

To meet the challenges of implementing effective progress monitoring, the Office of Special Education Programs has funded the National Center on Student Progress Monitoring. We are a national technical assistance and dissemination center dedicated to the implementation of scientifically based student progress monitoring (Grades K–5).

(Continued)

(Continued)

Research Institute on Progress Monitoring: www.progressmonitoring.net

The Office of Special Education Programs has funded the Research Institute on Progress Monitoring to develop a system of progress monitoring to evaluate effects of individualized instruction on access to and progress within the general education curriculum.

Schoolhouse Technologies: www.schoolhousetech.com

Printable Worksheets, Activities, and Tests for the Differentiated Classroom. Resource creation software for the differentiated classroom from Schoolhouse Technologies saves you the time to do what you do best—teach! Quickly and easily create printable worksheets, activities, and tests for a wide range of student levels and abilities. Now you can deliver an effective individualized educational experience—and have more time for teaching.

The Math Worksheet Site.com: http://themathworksheetsite.com

With The Math Worksheet Site you can create an endless supply of printable math worksheets. The intuitive interface gives you the ability to easily customize each worksheet to target your students' specific needs. Every worksheet is created when you request it, so they are different every time.

Yearly Progress Pro (McGraw-Hill): http://www.yearlyprogresspro.com

Yearly Progress Pro is a research-based assessment, instructional, and intervention tool that gives teachers and administrators specific frequent feedback on student progress; provides instant, automatic, on-the-spot intervention; and ensures that instruction is aligned to national and state standards.

Textbook Resource for All Aspects of CBM: www.guilford.com

Hosp, M. K., Hosp, J. L., & Howell, K. W. (2007). *The ABCs of CBM: A Practical Guide to Curriculum-Based Measurement.* New York: Guilford Press.

Note: This list is not intended to be comprehensive but rather includes resources we tend to use quite frequently in our own work and research relating to effective mathematics instruction.

IMPORTANCE OF THE CORE MATHEMATICS PROGRAM

Currently, a great deal of effort is directed toward Tier 2 and in many cases Tier 3 instructional programs and supports; in other words, students who are already struggling. Often, we hear the question, "What can I do with the students who are struggling in my math class?" Although an important question in any RTI model, by itself, this question implies a "remedial approach" and tends to focus on Tier 2 and/or Tier 3. The key phrase in this question is "students who are struggling . . ." An effective RTI model addresses students' instructional needs *before* (i.e., preventative) they begin to struggle as well as while they are struggling; in other words, educators need to carefully examine and scrutinize core mathematics programs, which include the curriculum and instruction provided in the general education mathematics classroom, Tier 1.

Since there is no "perfect" mathematics curriculum (despite publisher claims) and not all curricula are created equally, educators must carefully select core mathematics programs based on their students' instructional characteristics and the design of the program. The careful analysis of core mathematics programs cannot be overstated or emphasized enough. If a school selects a poorly designed core mathematics program (e.g., one that overemphasizes conceptual knowledge or one that overemphasizes procedural knowledge, or a student-centered curriculum vs. a teacher-directed curriculum), the foundation of the RTI model is already significantly weakened and likely to be less effective. The results of a poor core mathematics curriculum either by design and/or by implementation can lead to more and more students requiring Tier 2 and Tier 3 support (i.e., struggling—basic or below basic), resulting in an overloading of the system's resources.

Resources are limited, both in terms of personnel and materials. To maximize the effectiveness of Tier 2 and Tier 3 interventions, the core mathematics program must address the instructional needs of the majority of the students (i.e., 80% or more). In plain English, if your school's end-of-year mathematics performance as measured by your state's assessment is less than 80% successful (i.e., proficient or above), the first area to address is the core mathematics curriculum. This does not mean a completely new program, but rather a careful analysis of gaps within the program that can be supplemented either with teacher-created materials and/or supplemental programs.

For example, if a school's third-grade mathematics performance breaks down as follows: 5% advanced, 20% proficient, 30% basic, and 45% below basic, the core mathematics curriculum is effective with only 25% of your student population and therefore could overload Tier 2 and Tier 3 instructional capacity. In this situation, the core mathematics instructional program must be addressed before Tier 2 and Tier 3 are even discussed. The core mathematics curriculum that must be addressed includes the mathematics curriculum in kindergarten and first, second, and third grade. Although third-grade teachers generally receive the most scrutiny, the results of third-grade assessments are actually a direct result of the core mathematics instructional program that starts in kindergarten and continues all the way through third grade.

Until school systems implement the practice of devoting all or the majority of the resources to Tiers 2 and 3, it is no different than putting the proverbial "thumb" in the leaking dike; yes, the leak may temporarily be plugged, but down the line, the dam is likely to explode. This explosion, although delayed, generally appears in the middle school grades, and the long-term results negatively impact the success of students completing algebra. More information on core mathematics programs is provided in Chapter 3.

SUMMARY

In this chapter, we covered the essential components to consider when designing and implementing an RTI model in math, common approaches to RTI, progress monitoring, and the importance of the core mathematics program. The information in this chapter provides the essential foundations for an effective RTI model but is not sufficient to guarantee success. Ultimately, the quality of instruction provided to students is the most important variable to the success and/or failure of RTI.

A Tiered Approach to More Effective Mathematics Instruction 3

Positive results can be achieved in a reasonable time at accessible cost, but a consistent, wise, community-wide effort will be required.

—National Mathematics Advisory Panel Final Report (2008), p. 12

The organization of RTI rests on a tiered system to structure instruction and interventions based on student needs. As discussed in Chapter 2, there are two basic approaches to RTI: the problem-solving approach and the standard protocol approach. Within the problem-solving approach, teachers decide on specific interventions to help students learn better based on formative assessment information. Within the standard protocol approach, students move through preset tiered interventions based on summative assessment data. Both approaches have advantages but neither approach is endorsed over the other here. Rather, we help explain how to choose interventions for each student or students based on empirical data of the intervention. More important, we also explain research-supported best practices that help reduce intervention and special education placement.

RTI tiered systems vary from state to state and district to district. However, most include three levels of instruction and curriculum defined by time requirements, class or group size, and curricular needs. Within each level, instruction and curriculum are designed to improve math performance of each student. Because the demands and individualization increase per level, there are distinct differences between the tiers. Among these differences are group numbers (i.e., number of students), curriculum (e.g., Voyager Math or Connected Math Concepts) or math skills taught (e.g., problem solving, basic facts), the intended frequency and duration of the lessons (e.g., 3–5 days/week for 20–60 minutes), who delivers the instruction (e.g., regular, special educator, or interventionist), and how the curriculum will be taught (e.g., teacher led or student centered). What is similar between the tiers is that instruction and curriculum must be research and evidence supported, focused on the needs of the students, and be data driven in decision making. With math education research still underdeveloped in a number of areas, calling for evidence-supported curriculum and instruction for all math skills seems premature. In one district, a debate emerged about which of two programs should be used for their Tier 1 instruction. Disappointingly, for both camps, neither program was supported by valid research. As such, the district allowed schools to choose their math program (curriculum) but then mandated that certain instructional delivery practices be used no matter what program was chosen. Thus, discriminating curriculum from instruction allows us to differentiate what part of our planning is derived from research and what part is not. In the discussion of each tier of instruction, we will explain both curriculum and instruction (see Figure 3.1).

Figure 3.1 Critical Aspects of a Tiered Approach to an Effective Mathematics Program

Curriculum is defined as a sequential set of math skills and objectives that students are expected to learn.	Interventions are defined as a planned and organized change to a student's instruction and curriculum aimed at improving math performance. Pierangelo and Giuliani (2008) define intervention as "extra help or extra instruction that is targeted specifically to skills that a student has not acquired" (p. 80).	Instruction is defined as providing direction or guidance so that students learn how to do something.

RTI tiers are often conceptualized by a pyramid or taxonomy. At the base of the taxonomy represents what is considered the best curriculum and instruction for 80% of the population. The base is called Tier 1. In the middle is Tier 2, which represents the best instruction and curriculum for the students who are not succeeding adequately at Tier 1. At the top of the taxonomy is Tier 3. Tier 3 represents what is considered the best curriculum and instruction for students who did not succeed in Tier 1 and now are not succeeding in Tier 2. Tier 3 is reserved for students identified with learning disabilities or those with the most serious academic concerns. If you choose to restrict Tier 3 for those with disabilities, there should be approximately 5%–8% of students with learning disabilities (Geary, 2004) whose struggle in mathematics necessitates modifying standards. A four-tiered taxonomy provides a similar approach for Tier 1, but Tiers 2 and 3 provide varying intensities of intervention. Tier 4 is reserved for special education (see Figure 3.2). For more details on tiered systems, see the work of Mellard and Johnson (2008).

Figure 3.2   The Taxonomy of the Tiered System of Instruction

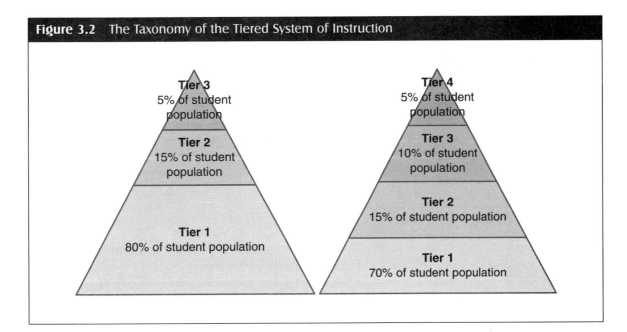

Before RTI can be considered, it is important to know what constitutes instruction and intervention in your school or district. Use the inventory chart (Table 3.1) to analyze what is currently used that may be employed in an RTI system. Does your school or district differentiate curriculum and instructional delivery based on the needs of students? Is there consistency among teachers and schools? Does your school or district have evidence to justify the use of the instructional delivery and curriculum? Is that evidence based on the performance of students, externally through peer-reviewed research, or both?

Table 3.1   Inventory Chart for Decisions Regarding Critical Aspects of a Tiered System

Curriculum		
General education curriculum per grade level	*External evidence of curriculum effectiveness*	*Internal evidence of curriculum effectiveness*
For struggling students curriculum per grade level	*External evidence of curriculum effectiveness*	*Internal evidence of curriculum effectiveness*
For special education nondiploma track curriculum per grade level	*External evidence of curriculum effectiveness*	*Internal evidence of curriculum effectiveness*

(Continued)

Table 3.1 (Continued)		
Instructional Implementation		
General education instructional components	*External evidence of instructional effectiveness*	*Internal evidence of instructional effectiveness*
For struggling students instructional components	*External evidence of instructional effectiveness*	*Internal evidence of instructional effectiveness*
Special education nondiploma track instructional components	*External evidence of instructional effectiveness*	*Internal evidence of instructional effectiveness*

Source: Witzel, B. S. (2009). *Response to Intervention in mathematics: Strategies for success.* Peterborough, NH: Staff Development for Educators. Reprinted with permission from Witzel.

Use your information from this inventory to identify what is necessary to use for each tiered instruction. Do not worry if you have blanks. Throughout this book, you will find new ideas to help you establish your instruction, curriculum, and interventions.

TIER 1 INSTRUCTION AND CURRICULUM

Tier 1 of RTI should be called Response to Instruction. Like all tiers, the purpose of Tier 1 is to help students achieve in mathematics. Tier 1 is to take place in the general education setting with the general education curriculum during a 50–60-minute uninterrupted time interval. To further understand Tier 1, it is important to examine both Tier 1 instruction and curriculum.

As is required within each tier, the curriculum must be research- or evidence-supported. In Tier 1, the general education curriculum should be supported by research. When starting a program, such research may be found through What Works Clearinghouse (www.whatworks.ed.org), for example, or peer-reviewed journals (e.g., *Learning Disabilities Research & Practice*, IES Practice guides, Center on Instruction), such as those endorsed and published by content-area organizations. Many publishers will show in-house studies of their curriculum or textbook and show results from districts. Be careful about declaring causation of such studies. There are often confounds within these studies that question the reported outcome. Also, with such a dearth of research on mathematics programs, it may be difficult to find valid research. Consequently, it is important to examine what is taught and, at a minimum, that your standards or expectations are addressed in a manner that brings the skills to mastery.

Once a curriculum has been in the school or district for a year or two, a statistical review of student performance should either support or refute the program (see Figure 3.3). If students who previously did not make progress are now making significant progress after implementation, the students should continue in the program. If students are still not making progress and you are relatively confident the program was implemented correctly and with fidelity, alternative programs should be discussed and considered. Recent research is bringing to light the fact that a math curriculum can have positive and negative effects on student performance. Review the effectiveness of your curriculum on the students.

Figure 3.3   One School's Program Evaluation

Tyler Middle School wanted to see if the students who participated in the new program improved over the previous 2 years. For each set of students (6th, 7th, and 8th grade), the average student score on the statewide exam decreased the year before the new program and increased significantly the year after implementation. Program evaluations like this one helped the school make the decision to keep the new program.

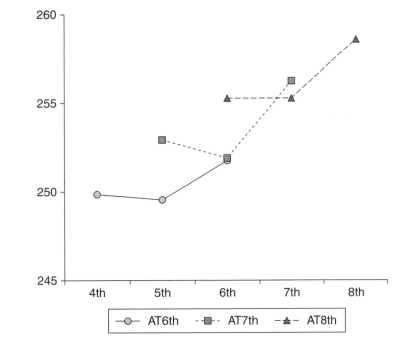

6th grade

Before Implementation: From 4th to 5th grade, the students at Albemarle decreased 0.31 points.

After Implementation: From 5th to 6th grade, the students at Albemarle increased 2.13 points.

(Continued)

Figure 3.3 (Continued)

7th grade

Before Implementation: From 5th to 6th grade, the students at Albemarle decreased 0.96 points.

After Implementation: From 6th to 7th grade, the students at Albemarle increased 4.14 points.

8th grade

Before Implementation: From 6th to 7th grade, the students at Albemarle increased 0.05 points.

After Implementation: From 7th to 8th grade, the students at Albemarle increased 3.29 points.

> What Works Clearinghouse (WWC) is a comprehensive list of summative research support for most major curricular and interventions that are available for purchase. The contributors to WWC evaluate the research outcomes and protocol. Each analysis includes the program description, effectiveness, and references.

> Tier I instruction cannot be what has always been done or what is most convenient for the teacher.

There are a number of resources available for investigating research on math programs. Assessment before and during implementation is vital to ongoing success and improvements.

Along with curriculum, Tier 1 should also include researched instruction. It is not enough to have a "good" textbook or an appropriately sequenced and coherent set of state standards. Teachers need to be able to deliver the curriculum effectively. Effective delivery requires that teachers aim to teach every student based on his or her individual needs. Tier 1 instruction should not be what has "always" been done or what is most convenient for the teacher or scheduling purposes. Rather, it is instructing the curriculum in a manner that meets the needs of the students in the classroom. Some ideas that may be used in Tier 1 are differentiation by class configurations, providing extra assistance, and peer groupings. The main point is that differentiation in Tier 1 is about what students need in order to succeed.

Classroom Scenario: Using Small Groups to Provide Additional Instructional Opportunities

In Mrs. Robles's fifth-grade math class, she teaches 18 students. Of the 18, 16 performed below average on last year's statewide math exam, and overall she believes that the students do not maintain an adequate amount of attention during whole-class instructional time. Two students in particular struggle significantly in class. They do not perform well in multiple-step problems and still have difficulty recalling their basic math facts. To help these two students in her classroom, she arranges desks into five small groups of four desks. Students are grouped in mixed-ability teams that rotate about the classroom during math class performing different subskills during short intervals. She still has a group instruction time, but performs it briefly before class and reinforces it and practices it during one of the group activities as the students rotate. When students need extra help, she calls them over to a help area in the classroom to receive the needed instruction. Additionally, she employs peer tutoring whereby pairs of students with slightly mixed achievement teach each other in the areas of their personal math weakness using the practice guide within her general curriculum.

Although this class keeps Mrs. Robles busy, she is much more comfortable planning effective instruction than having to stamp out disruptions that used to occupy significant amounts of her time and energy. Each component of her instruction of the general education curriculum is considered Tier 1 instruction because students are still on grade level in her class.

TIER 2 INTERVENTION AND CURRICULUM

Key components of Tier 2 interventions, as defined by Pierangelo and Giuliani (2008), include the size of the instructional group, mastery requirement of content, frequency of progress monitoring, duration of the intervention, frequency with which the intervention is delivered, and instructor considerations. Tier 2 is considered the first line of intervention for students not meeting benchmark standards (Hall, 2008). The list of instructional resources for math at the end of this chapter provides additional resources for effective mathematics instruction in Tier 2.

Size of the Instructional Group

Reducing the group size in Tier 2 allows the teacher more flexible groupings. Grouping can lead to increased engagement and motivation as well as more individualized mathematics support. Small-group work allows for more student responses and teacher feedback, whereas whole-class instruction enables a shared learning environment with more normative analysis. Along with instructional reasons, reduced class size may allow the teacher to implement more intensive curricula that might require time-consuming or rigorous procedures.

Mastery Requirement of Content

It is important that an intervention leads students to success in areas where they were previously weak. Many of the mathematics programs available today introduce a math concept only to skip to a different math concept a day or two later. The idea of skipping around within content is to help students see the interconnectedness of multiple math skills. This approach has been called a spiral curriculum. While this approach might enable students to see how ideas are related, it may conversely cause difficulty for students trying to master a single concept and related skill. Any program that does not focus on students learning a core math skill should be avoided for Tier 2 intervention. Instead, an intervention curriculum should lead students to mastery of math skills.

Frequency of Progress Monitoring

The effectiveness of an assessment should be monitored closely. A progress-monitoring protocol that includes assessment frequent enough to make informed and student-centered decisions is important to any intervention system.

Duration of the Intervention

Based on the effectiveness of the intervention, the duration of an intervention is dependent on student outcomes. Once the intervention is determined to have been or is or is not being effective, a decision must be made as to the next step with the student.

Frequency of the Intervention

Intervention curricula should be used continuously and frequently to ensure that student work from one day to the next is fluid. If the approach is implemented inconsistently, then student outcomes will likely appear inconsistent to the apparent in-class successfulness.

Instructor Considerations

The instructor who implements the intervention strategy must be qualified to provide the intervention. Thus, the person must be trained in the intervention and know the content of the intervention. Additionally, the person must understand assessment and child development such that he or she can make appropriate adjustments to the instruction necessary to deliver the particular curriculum that the student is learning.

Tier 2 instruction and curriculum are designed for flexible groups of six to eight students who are working on the same skill areas, 4 to 5 days a week for 20–30 minutes. Small-group instruction is preferred in that it allows for more individualization of student responses and thus more frequent assessment to drive the instruction. Skill deficits are the same for curricular reasons in that Tier 2 complements the general education curriculum. Typical Tier 2 curriculum may entail such math skills as computational fluency, number sense, problem solving, or fractions. These skill areas should fill gaps within the students' learning that hinder their performance in the general education mathematics curriculum. Tier 2 should be taught in a separate setting for most of the week in a time period that allows for the intervention to be delivered.

Tier 2 is not a homework session or study hall where students practice what was learned in the general education classroom. Rather, Tier 2 is separate and additional to the general education curriculum and, most important, includes teacher-led explicit instruction.

An example of Tier 2 is found in Mr. Dobbins's room. As a sixth-grade teacher, he has the responsibility of teaching one class of seven students who struggle in mathematics as shown on the first-quarter benchmark test. This group of students struggles in computation, which has interfered with their ability to perform well in multiple-step problems and fractions computation. Additionally, they are weaker in place value knowledge, so computation appears even weaker when working with multidigit numbers. During this brief class period, he teaches accurate computation with multidigit numbers using the concrete-to-representational-to-abstract sequence of instruction (see Chapter 5 for more information) and then works on fluency using computer-based instruction (see Chapter 7 for more information). After the first quarter, six of the seven students improved in both place value knowledge and computation and in the general education classroom. Of those six, four met benchmarks on the quarterly assessment. Thus, those four no longer require intervention. The other two students will continue in Tier 2 interventions to improve further in general education. The seventh student who is not improving in the general education setting (Tier 1) or with the interventions (Tier 2) will receive additional and different interventions and will be closely monitored to possibly go for testing for special education (Tier 3).

In Chapters 5 through 9, we describe Tier 2 interventions for some of the most historically difficult math topics (number sense, fact fluency, fractions and decimals, problem solving, and vocabulary). Each of the strategies in these chapters varies by level of intensity and can be used in a Tier 2 setting.

TIER 3 INSTRUCTION AND CURRICULUM

Students who receive Tier 3 interventions or alternate instruction are students who are performing below standards and have not adequately responded to Tier 1 instruction or Tier 2 intervention. For many researchers and practitioners, Tier 3 instruction is also thought of as special education (Mellard & Johnson, 2008) and as such, a full psychoeducational battery of tests should be considered before a student begins Tier 3 intervention.

Students in Tier 3 typically do not have one or two subskill deficits in mathematics, like they would at Tier 2. Rather, the deficits appear across the content area or areas. Tier 3 is designed to replace the general education curriculum and instruction. Thus, Tier 3 is different. It is more intense in student participation and interaction and more personalized to the specific needs of the students. Tier 3 math curriculum should be taught 5 days a week for 60–90 minutes a day.

If a student is not achieving in the general education curriculum despite evidence-based and research-supported instruction and interventions, then it is important to consider the transition needs of the student. What are appropriate and essential life skills and employment skills that can be met in the math class that will help the student in the future? This individually designed curriculum might not be necessarily based on state standards but rather on transition needs. To develop a Tier 3 curriculum or sequential stepwise approach aimed at transition outcomes, teachers might use task analysis, such as OPTIMIZE (Witzel & Riccomini, 2007). OPTIMIZE is explained in Chapter 4.

An example of Tier 3 instruction and curriculum appears in Ms. Richardson's high school math class. The students are not on a diploma track but instead have individualized transition goals. Ms. Richardson had the students start a cookie company. The students worked in teams to create the name of the company, teamed with a marketing class to develop a logo and advertising, and then set up recipes. The recipes produced small samples, which were calculated by proportions and fractions, and the students tested their potential products.

SUMMARY

In this chapter, preparations for RTI in math were introduced. Students who need special instruction cannot wait until RTI is announced. An efficient plan must be in place that recognizes the purpose of each tier and describes what will happen within each school. This plan must take into account the effects of both curriculum and instruction on student learning so that appropriate interventions may be prepared. RTI isn't simply another special education legislation that can be handled by another page on the IEP. RTI is a ship that carries with it a mandate to all in education to do what everyone says is their goal: teach so that all students can learn to the best of their ability.

Instructional Resources for Math

The following is a list of instructional resources for mathematics to assist in planning, designing, and implementing instructional supports in Tiers 1–3:

Center on Instruction: www.centeroninstruction.org

The Center on Instruction offers materials and resources on mathematics to build educators' knowledge of instruction for students with low achievement in mathematics, improve professional development models for math teachers, and build teachers' skills in monitoring student growth toward important math outcomes.

The Access Center: Improving Outcomes for All Students K–8: www.k8accesscenter.org

Our resources focus on core content areas—language arts, math, and science—as well as on instructional and learning strategies to provide students with disabilities access to rigorous academic content. We have a series of professional development modules and information briefs on such topics as teaching and learning strategies, media and materials, supports and accommodations, universal design for learning, differentiated instruction, and collaborative teaching.

LD Online: www.ldonline.org

LD Online seeks to help children and adults reach their full potential by providing accurate and up-to-date information and advice about learning disabilities and ADHD. The site features hundreds of helpful articles, multimedia, monthly columns by noted experts, first-person essays, children's writing and artwork, a comprehensive resource guide, very active forums, and a Yellow Pages referral directory of professionals, schools, and products.

MathVIDS: http://www.coedu.usf.edu/main/departments/sped/mathvids/index.html

MathVIDS is an interactive Web site for teachers who are teaching mathematics to struggling learners and is made possible through funding by the Virginia Department of Education. The primary theme of MathVIDS is to help educators connect why struggling learners have difficulty learning mathematics to effective instructional practices for these students.

National Council of Teachers of Mathematics: http://www.nctm.org

The National Council of Teachers of Mathematics is a public voice of mathematics education, providing vision, leadership, and professional development to support teachers in ensuring equitable mathematics learning of the highest quality for all students.

Direct Instruction Textbook Resource

Stein, M., Kinder, D., Silbert, J., & Carnine, D. (2006). *Designing Effective Mathematics Instruction: A Direct Instruction Approach* (4th ed.). Upper Saddle River, NJ: Pearson Education, Inc.

What Works Clearinghouse: www.whatworks.ed.gov

An initiative of the U.S. Department of Education's Institute of Education Sciences, the WWC:

- Produces user-friendly practice guides for educators that address instructional challenges with research-based recommendations for schools and classrooms
- Assesses the rigor of research evidence on the effectiveness of interventions (programs, products, practices, and policies), giving educators the tools to make informed decisions
- Develops and implements standards for reviewing and synthesizing education research
- Provides a public and easily accessible registry of education evaluation researchers to assist schools, school districts, and program developers with designing and carrying out rigorous evaluations

Best Evidence Encyclopedia: www.bestevidence.org

The Best Evidence Encyclopedia is a free Web site created by the Johns Hopkins University School of Education's Center for Data-Driven Reform in Education (CDDRE) under funding from the Institute of Education Sciences, U.S. Department of Education. It is intended to give educators and researchers fair and useful information about the strength of the evidence supporting a variety of programs available for students in Grades K–12.

Note: This list is not intended to be comprehensive but rather includes resources we tend to use quite frequently in our own work and research relating to effective mathematics instruction.

Mathematics Interventions Overview 4

Mathematics interventions delivered in an RTI framework can have a positive effect on student learning. It is important to choose appropriate interventions and deliver the interventions wisely in order to have the desired effect. If math interventions are developed and the time is used inappropriately, then RTI will be the failure, not the student. It is our belief that if Tier 2 or 3 intervention time is used for homework or extra independent practice only, then RTI is a waste of time. Moreover, if an ineffective curriculum is selected and/or is taught by an ill-informed or unprepared teacher, then RTI is a waste of time. More accurately, instruction and intervention are not possible.

> The NMAP recommends that those responsible for math education have strong math skills.

Mathematics interventions should be taught daily using systematic, explicit, and research-supported instruction and curriculum that includes ongoing assessment and progress monitoring tailored to the specific areas of weakness of each student. By placing students in small groups for Tiers 2 and 3, the instructional delivery options increase. As students are placed into increasing tiers, group size must decrease in order to best meet the individual needs of each student. In small groups, students may be peer grouped and called on individually more often to increase interactions, individualized feedback, and informal assessment. Additionally, decreasing the size of the group allows for easier adaptation of curricular content.

For example, in a class of 25 students, the teacher may spend a great deal of effort and time making certain that everyone is on the same page and accomplishing the same task. When a small group of students are not keeping up or are unable to keep up, it is more difficult to recognize the errors being made and make immediate adjustments for those select few students, all the while keeping the rest of the class at their same pace. In a Tier 2 class of six students, the teacher is more likely to notice the difficulty of a particular student and make immediate adjustments to the instruction so that the student can acquire the skill. In Tier 3, class and group size are even smaller, and thus curriculum, instruction, and assessment are individualized to the specific and immediate need of each student.

Math intervention research has grown in recent years since RTI was first endorsed in government white papers and then with the Individuals with Disabilities Education Act (IDEA) of 2004. As such, some research projects have made claims of being an effective Tier 2 intervention while others have claimed effectiveness for *all* students in Tier 1. Because of the various claims, research reported in this book will use research that supports whole-class curriculum and instruction for struggling students to constitute Tier 1 instruction and research that focuses on small-group curriculum and instruction to constitute intervention research. The focus of this book is to prevent a learning disabilities diagnosis by using highly effective intervention methods. As such, Tier 3 modifications are looked at as more intense renditions of the interventions. Because the focus of RTI is on prevention of disabilities, alternative graduation curriculum, nondiploma track, and work study interventions are not the focus of the interventions explored in this document.

WHO NEEDS INTERVENTION?

We must consider a number of factors when concerning ourselves with who requires intervention in math. Many people focus on struggling groups such as those with a low socioeconomic status (SES), females, those with memory issues, or those who are hyperactive. In reality, it is highly unlikely that any person will never struggle in mathematics. Mathematics, unlike other content areas, is very complex and ever increasing in difficulty and demand. So it is important to look at screening data and make individual recommendations accordingly. Extra attention should be given to the grade level of the struggling student. If a kindergartner or second-grade student is struggling in math early on in their academic career, then the need for intervention is urgent. Weaknesses in early learning concepts can interfere with future math performance. Students who struggle early require immediate and effective interventions to prepare for future success. While the need for early intervention is important, it does not negate the need for intervention of students in upper elementary to secondary levels. In fact, as students progress in grade level, mathematics difficulties become more complex, which requires more complex and intensive interventions.

WHAT DO I TEACH FOR THE INTERVENTION?

Some assessment batteries will help pinpoint specific areas of weakness for students. Knowing exactly in what to intervene is a key to successful intervention. While some assessment batteries provide a detailed picture, other assessment batteries do not. Assessment batteries that provide a percentile or rating only do not provide guidance as to what to intervene in but rather to whom the intervention should occur.

Typical areas of mathematics intervention research, as identified in preassessments, cover the topics of number sense, computation, fractions/decimals/proportions, algebraic equations, and problem solving. Students who exhibit math difficulties early struggle in understanding and task performance with number sense concepts such as counting, quantification or magnitude of number, number-to-numeral identification, base 10 and place value, and fluent arithmetic strategies. Students who continue to struggle in mathematics require intervention in fractions, computation, and problem solving. If problems persist into middle school, interventions with algebraic concepts, such as solving equations; continued work on fractions, decimals, and proportions; along with computation involving negatives are important.

WHO SHOULD INTERVENE?

At any school, the person who is intervening with the students may be a general or special education teacher, a mathematics coach, a mathematic supervisor, or even an instructional assistant (Gersten et al., 2009). No matter who is delivering the intervention, that person requires training in the intervention curriculum, the instructional delivery most effective for the student, and the assessment procedures to best ensure informed instruction for the student. Additionally, the interventionist must possess curricular and content knowledge of the grade level of at least the year before and after the student's current

> "Substantial differences in mathematics achievement of students are attributable to differences in teachers. Teachers are crucial to students' opportunities to learn and to their learning of mathematics."
>
> —NMAP (2008)

grade and curricular placement so as to make proper goals for the student and work with the material to which the student already has been introduced.

WHERE?

An area free of distractions is required for the intervention. Students with attention or peer pressure concerns require the ability to be allowed to focus on the work and not on others' behavior. For example, a former recess closet accessible only to the outside with one wall conveniently used for ball play by a couple hundred children every afternoon is not appropriate. Special education has come a long way in the past two decades to move special education classes to classes that, at the least, appear like those in the rest of the school. It is conceivable that broom closets would be reopened to provide interventions. Instead of looking for a convenient location, it is better to find the most effective place for students to learn. Although six students and a teacher could fit in a former book room, it is not always conducive to learning. The best place for interventions to take place is an area that is free of distractions, capable of handling and displaying technology appropriate for the selected interventions, and large enough to allow necessary instructional groupings, movement, and interactions. Some example seating arrangements taken from the IRIS Center (n.d.) are displayed in Figure 4.1.

Figure 4.1 Example Seating Arrangements for Class Instruction and Small-Group Intervention

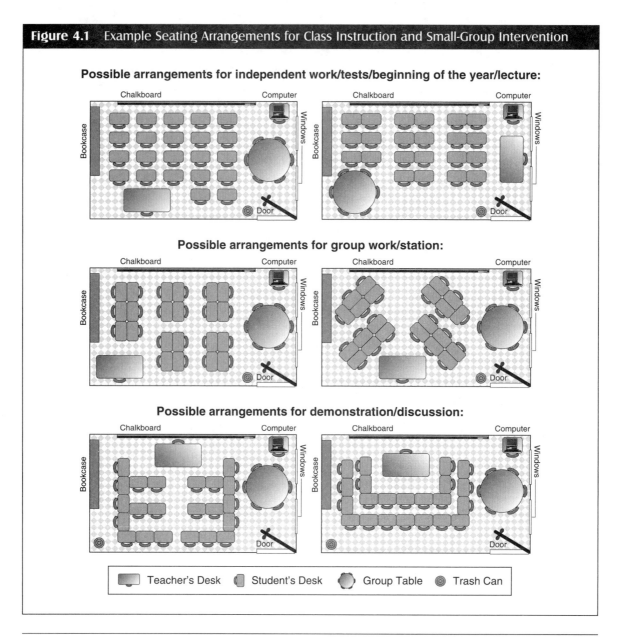

Source: Courtesy of the IRIS Center, Peabody College.

HOW LONG?

Interventions should happen 4–5 days per week for a minimum of 20 minutes. Considerable research conducted across many years has consistently demonstrated improved student achievement through the increase of instructional time (Ellis, Worthington, & Larkin, 1994). Although no absolute time recommendations exist, the recommendations that we put forth should be considered starting points and should only increase. Student attention span and instructional delivery will cause fluctuations in the actual time for intervention. Some interventions are preset to last up to 50 minutes for middle school classes. This is fine, but make certain that the delivery varies the activities quickly and maintains frequent interactions to help keep the students focused. The intervention set should occur until the students meet grade-level expectations or the students are assessed to need more intensive instruction.

What kinds of instructional delivery work best with interventions?

> Instructional practice should be informed by high-quality research, when available, and by the best professional judgment and experience of accomplished classroom teachers. High-quality research does not support the contention that instruction should be either entirely "student-centered" or "teacher-directed." Research indicates that some forms of particular instructional practices can have a positive impact under specified conditions. (NMAP, 2008, p. 11)

Students who struggle in mathematics require explicit and systematic instruction (Gersten et al., 2009). Such instruction should be provided in all tiers for struggling students. However, while there are many similarities between tiered instructional deliveries, the extra time allotted in each successive tier provides additional classroom opportunities. Gersten and his colleagues suggest that educators use the time opportunities to provide extra practice and more interactions through the use of clear examples and models, more detailed feedback, and extra and different use of think alouds. The think alouds that are recommended for the teacher to use in Tier 1 can be used more extensively in Tier 2. Not only should teachers use think alouds, but the students should as well. Verbalizations of thought process and understanding have a history of research effectiveness, particularly for students with learning disabilities (Baker, Gersten, & Scanlon, 2002).

Using teacher think alouds can be an awkward means of teaching for someone who is unfamiliar with the process and the research. However, it is highly effective, particularly for students who have not established a means to approach a problem. Thus, it is important for teachers to learn this skill. There are a couple of things to keep in mind when implementing think alouds. The first is that you need to have developed a clear and simple set of sequenced procedures that solves the problem (and hopefully several problems like it). Next, when implementing, it is good to go through at least one whole problem aloud first without student interaction. The students need to see the problem solving in its entirety. Also, depending on the students, you will have to scaffold the steps individually or in groups so that they can be repeated. Finally, provide practice so that the students can name the steps and think aloud accurately and independently.

In Figure 4.2, the teacher is at an intermediate step in showing an integer method for subtraction without regrouping. It is important to verbalize the reasoning rather than simply reading the problem as it would be written on a board. Once a teacher models a problem using a think aloud, he should ask the students to repeat the thought process. This extra step adds instructional time, but the additional interactions are valuable when teaching students who have a history of memorization difficulties.

Figure 4.2 A Stepwise Example of Teacher and Student Think Alouds to Solve a Problem Using an Integer Method

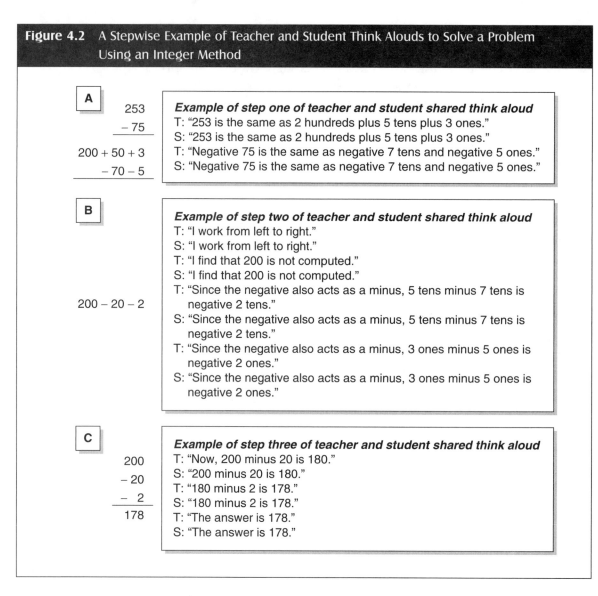

A

$$253$$
$$-\ 75$$

$$200 + 50 + 3$$
$$-\ 70 - 5$$

Example of step one of teacher and student shared think aloud

T: "253 is the same as 2 hundreds plus 5 tens plus 3 ones."
S: "253 is the same as 2 hundreds plus 5 tens plus 3 ones."
T: "Negative 75 is the same as negative 7 tens and negative 5 ones."
S: "Negative 75 is the same as negative 7 tens and negative 5 ones."

B

$$200 - 20 - 2$$

Example of step two of teacher and student shared think aloud

T: "I work from left to right."
S: "I work from left to right."
T: "I find that 200 is not computed."
S: "I find that 200 is not computed."
T: "Since the negative also acts as a minus, 5 tens minus 7 tens is negative 2 tens."
S: "Since the negative also acts as a minus, 5 tens minus 7 tens is negative 2 tens."
T: "Since the negative also acts as a minus, 3 ones minus 5 ones is negative 2 ones."
S: "Since the negative also acts as a minus, 3 ones minus 5 ones is negative 2 ones."

C

$$200$$
$$-\ 20$$
$$-\ 2$$
$$\overline{178}$$

Example of step three of teacher and student shared think aloud

T: "Now, 200 minus 20 is 180."
S: "200 minus 20 is 180."
T: "180 minus 2 is 178."
S: "180 minus 2 is 178."
T: "The answer is 178."
S: "The answer is 178."

Along the line of increasing frequency of interactions, teachers can use several forms of simple and advanced technology to increase student participation in class. One of the more recent technologies to make it to the classroom is an interactive whiteboard. The SMART Board and other interactive board technologies have options for student input in a couple of formats. Students can answer multiguess questions from a portable keypad, or they can write directly on a portable notepad allowing their original work to be displayed. Contrary to the belief that open discussions can hurt a student's feelings thus causing their work effort to disintegrate, when handled correctly, discussing a student's work can provide the student with clear explanations from other students. In many cases, students are more resistant to teacher feedback than they are to peer feedback. Students need to be taught how to provide constructive and supportive feedback in order to make this work.

Along the lines of increasing peer interactions and appropriate peer feedback, the use of peer-assisted learning strategies (PALS) has had great success in mathematics and reading. Specific to the mathematics, Fuchs, Fuchs, and Karns (2001) found success across achievement levels in kindergartners when PALS was implemented. PALS is enacted by pairing two students of slightly different achievement for 30 minutes three to four times a week. If there are an uneven number of students, then flexible groups of three are a possibility. The intervention is focused on practice of ideas already taught to the students. Each intervention is individually arranged according to the student's needs. Each member of the pair plays the role of coach and student in a reciprocal role play. Additionally, each member of the team is involved in progress monitoring. To learn more about PALS mathematics research, visit the site http://kc.vanderbilt .edu/pals/library/mathres.html.

HOW DO I ORGANIZE MY CURRICULUM?

Information from assessments should provide the teacher/interventionist with a focused outcome on what the student is lacking that may be preventing success in the general education curriculum. With this focused outcome in mind, the teacher can design curricular steps to help the student reach that goal. One such way to break down instruction is through task analysis. Task analysis has long been recognized as a means for taking large and difficult tasks and breaking them down into reasonable, sequential, and learnable chunks (Witzel & Riccomini, 2007). In special education, task analysis has been used for low-incidence special education populations to teach life and work skills. The teacher would start by teaching a small first step of the sequence of things someone must learn. For grade-level mathematics, the approach is similar. With a typical second-grade standard of two-digit addition and subtraction, students must not only know addition and subtraction facts but also know the reasoning behind addition and subtraction and place value in preparation for regrouping and borrowing. To best instruct a standard like two-digit addition and subtraction, teachers need to task analyze the standard to ensure that students are prepared for success and to appropriately teach *all* precursor skills. Some teachers in Tier 1 elect not to task analyze their curriculum to minute steps because of reasons such as concern with instructional time or demands made by preset pacing guides. However, because Tiers 2 and 3 provide more instructional time and many of the intervention curricula available do not incorporate a rigid pacing guide, teachers are more able to task analyze curriculum into "baby steps" to best meet the learning needs of struggling students.

One strategy to help teachers and curricular analysts task analyze a curriculum to more accurately reach a desired outcome and best meet the needs of students is through the use of OPTIMIZE (Riccomini, Witzel, & Riccomini, in press; Witzel & Riccomini, 2007). The eight steps of OPTIMIZE help teachers examine and revise their current curriculum to fill in gaps or reduce unnecessarily spiraled activities. The steps of OPTIMIZE are:

1. O—Organize the math skills of a textbook chapter before teaching.

2. P—Pair your sequence with that of the textbook.

3. T—Take note of the commonalities and differences.

4. I—Inspect earlier chapters and later chapters to see if they cover the differences.

5. M—Match supplemental guides to see if they cover the differences.

6. I—Identify additional instruction to complement the current text/ curriculum.

7. Z—Zero in on the optimal sequence with your new knowledge.

8. E—Evaluate and improve the sequence every year.

See the example in Table 4.1 that demonstrates how to enact OPTIMIZE with your curriculum. In this example, a Tier 2 interventionist, Mrs. Hunt, tackles the demand of intervening with a group of students to learn the above-mentioned skill, two-digit addition and subtraction. Reviewing the textbook,

Table 4.1 Example Application of OPTIMIZE to Instructional Sequence for an Algebra Chapter

Textbook Chapter Sequence	*Alternative Textbook*	*New Instructional Sequence*
1. Comparing real numbers on a number line	1. Ordering real numbers on a number line	1. Pretest for knowledge of integers
2. Adding integers on a number line	2. Adding integers with positive addends	2. Ordering integers
3. Subtracting integers on a number line	3. Adding and subtracting integers with negative and positive addends	3. Adding integers on a number line
4. Adding and subtracting in a matrix	4. Multiplying and dividing integers with one positive product or quotient	4. Adding and subtracting integers on a number line
5. Multiplying integers	5. Multiplying and dividing integers with two negative or positive addends or quotients	5. Rules for positive and negative terms
6. Using the distributive property to simplify expressions		6. Multiplying and dividing integers
7. Dividing real numbers to simplify expressions	6. Application of integers in real-life scenarios	7. Application with distributive property and expressions
8. Solving the probability of an event		*Note:* Include real-life scenarios throughout unit and include maintenance of each successive skill per chapter.

Note: This is just one example sequence and should not be interpreted as the only or correct sequence. The instructional sequence is dependent on state standards, access to curriculum and materials, and, most important, the students' instructional needs. OPTIMIZE was developed by Witzel & Riccomini (2007).

Mrs. Hunt observes several extraneous skills like spatial relations and telling time. Since these are important topics, they can be used as tools to teach this skill rather than as separate lessons. Additionally, this textbook alternated addition and subtraction several times. While examining the alternate textbook, she finds fewer extraneous math skills, but that textbook did not include some ideas, such as fact families. Instead of choosing one textbook or the other, Mrs. Hunt task analyzes a sequence of math skills that leads directly to two-digit addition and subtraction. Her delivery of this task analysis in a Tier 2 setting requires Mrs. Hunt to assess where students are along the task analysis to better know where to start in the sequence.

WHAT TYPES OF CURRICULAR STRATEGIES SHOULD BE USED FOR TIER 2 AND TIER 3 INTERVENTIONS?

There are several instructional approaches that can be used to present curriculum at the Tier 2 or 3 level. Research is in its infancy, but sufficient evidence is emerging to preliminarily endorse certain intervention strategies. Among the research-supported and evidence-supported approaches are explicit instruction for word problems (Wilson & Sindelar, 1991) and computation (Tournaki, 2003), use of visual representations for word problems (Owen & Fuchs, 2002), schema-based problem solving for word problems (Xin, Jitendra, & Deatline-Buchman, 2005), the concrete to representational to abstract (CRA) sequence of instruction for fractions (Butler, Miller, Crehan, Babbitt, & Pierce, 2003), algebra (Witzel, 2005; Witzel, Mercer, & Miller, 2003) and computation (Miller & Mercer, 1993), and meta-cognitive strategy instruction for fraction computation (Hutchinson, 1993). Moreover, in meta-analyses of research findings from studies during the past three decades, Baker, Gersten, and Lee (2002) as well as the National Mathematics Advisory Panel (2008) and RTI Math Practice Guide Panel (Gersten et al., 2009) support these instructional and curriculum interventions.

The repeated conclusion that visual and concrete representations should be incorporated in instruction should not be overlooked. CRA and visual representations are very important strategies for teaching students to learn complex tasks. The NMAP (2008) and RTI Math Practice Guide Panel (Gersten et al., 2009) both supported the use of CRA based on its significant effect size. CRA is a three-stage process of learning whereby students first learn by interacting with concrete objects (see Figure 4.3). Then they use the same steps to solve the problem using pictorial representations. Finally, the students use the same steps again to solve the problem using the abstract or Arabic symbols. It is important to use the same steps for each stage of learning so that students learn the procedures to solving problems.

Some teachers may find it difficult to locate manipulatives that can be used in the manner in which CRA is founded. If so, the National Library of Virtual Manipulatives (NLVM) can be used as a resource to help the teacher peruse the

Figure 4.3 The CRA Sequence of Instruction

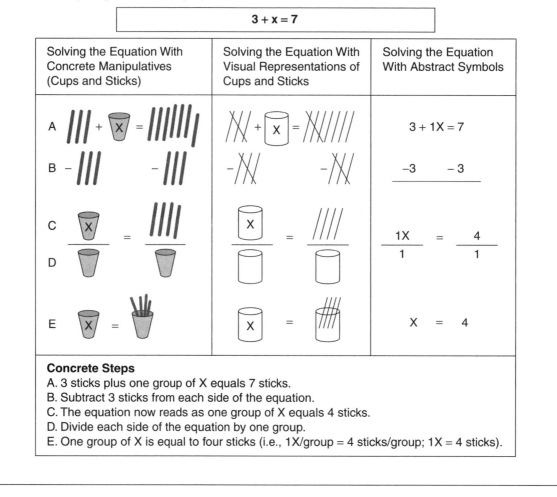

Example 8. A set of matched concrete, visual, and abstract representations to teach solving single-variable equations

$$3 + x = 7$$

Solving the Equation With Concrete Manipulatives (Cups and Sticks)	Solving the Equation With Visual Representations of Cups and Sticks	Solving the Equation With Abstract Symbols

Concrete Steps
A. 3 sticks plus one group of X equals 7 sticks.
B. Subtract 3 sticks from each side of the equation.
C. The equation now reads as one group of X equals 4 sticks.
D. Divide each side of the equation by one group.
E. One group of X is equal to four sticks (i.e., 1X/group = 4 sticks/group; 1X = 4 sticks).

Source: Gersten, R., Beckmann, S., Clarke, B., Foegen, A., Marsh, L., Star, J. R., & Witzel, B. (2009). *Assisting students struggling with mathematics: Response to Intervention (RTI) for elementary and middle schools* (NCEE 2009-4060). Washington, DC: National Center for Education Evaluation and Regional Assistance, Institute of Education Sciences, U.S. Department of Education. Retrieved from http://ies.ed.gov/ncee/wwc/publications/practiceguides.

use of manipulatives (see Figure 4.4). In each math strand and grade-level band, teachers can review several manipulatives designed to help students learn concretely. Once found, the teacher can obtain the manipulatives and use them in a CRA sequence.

The interventions in Chapters 6 through 9 will depict how to enact these curricular strategies with the specific areas of math weakness that are found to be most prevalent with students at risk for learning disabilities in mathematics: number sense, fact computation, fractions and decimals, and problem solving.

Figure 4.4 Sample Manipulative View From the National Library of Virtual Manipulatives (NLVM)

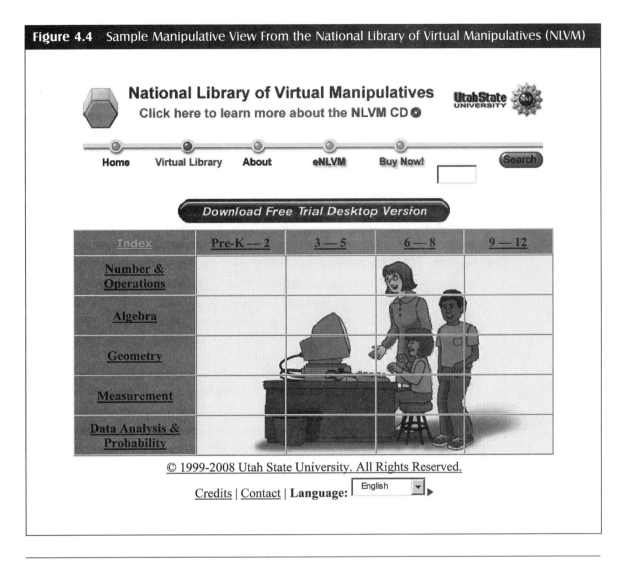

SUMMARY

Students who exhibit repeated difficulties in math require a different mode of instruction. A knowledgeable interventionist using evidence-supported curricula should explicitly teach deficit skills to mastery in hopes of curbing each student's poor performance. The intervention should cease when assessment data show that the student has begun to succeed in mathematics or when the assessment data show that it is time for more intensive intervention. There are several interventions from which interventionists may choose. It is important to choose interventions for their curriculum support and necessary instructional delivery. The next four chapters will focus on key areas frequently requiring interventions: number sense, computational fluency, fractions and decimals, and problem solving.

List of Mathematics Interventions and Programs

Peer-Assisted Learning Strategies: http://kc.vanderbilt.edu/pals

PALS Reading and PALS Math were developed to help teachers accommodate diverse learners and to promote their academic success. PALS is listed among the best evidence-supported math programs on the Johns Hopkins University Web site, Best Evidence Encyclopedia (BEE). The What Works Clearinghouse found "The Peer-Assisted Learning Strategies© instructional program to have potentially positive effects on reading achievement" for elementary-age ELL children. For information specifically about Hot Math and other Tier 1 and 2 interventions, contact flora .murray@vanderbilt.edu.

Hot Math: Problem-Solving Program

Hot Math is available in a manual that includes teaching scripts for implementing all five units and provides all necessary materials (e.g., posters, overheads, worked problems, classroom exercises, scoring keys, homework assignments, personal charts, class charts). For information specifically about Hot Math and other Tier 1 and Tier 2 interventions, contact flora.murray@vanderbilt.edu.

Otter Creek Institute: http://www.oci-sems.com

A leading provider in high-quality training and resources, Otter Creek is dedicated to the success of our nation's teachers and students. Specific instructional interventions for Writing Numerals, Mastering Math Facts, and Problem-Solving Strategy Instruction.

Voyageur Learning-VMath: http://www.voyagerlearning.com/vmath/index.jsp

Many students need extra support to succeed in math and pass high-stakes tests. VMath fills critical learning gaps with a balanced, systematic approach, combining print materials, robust assessment, and online technology to create confident, independent learners in math.

Computation of Fractions: Math Intervention for Elementary and Middle Grades Students: http://www.pearsonhighered.com/educator

This intervention is based on the CRA instructional sequence and contains 30 instructional lessons, pretest, and posttest to determine effectiveness. The effectiveness of this instructional sequence is supported by research in which certified teachers provided daily whole-class and/or small-group instruction using concrete manipulative objects, then pictorial representations, and finally abstract representations of fractions.

Computation of Integers: Math Intervention for Elementary and Middle Grades Students: http://www.pearsonhighered.com/educator

This intervention is based on the CRA instructional sequence and contains 30 instructional lessons, pretest, and posttest to determine effectiveness. The effectiveness of this instructional sequence is supported by research in which certified teachers provided daily whole-class and/or small-group instruction using concrete manipulative objects, then pictorial representations, and finally abstract representations of positive and negative integers.

Computation of Simple Equations: Math Intervention for Middle Grade Students: http://www.pearsonhighered.com/educator

This intervention is based on the CRA instructional sequence and contains 30 instructional lessons, pretest, and posttest to determine effectiveness. The effectiveness of this instructional sequence is supported by research in which certified teachers provided daily whole-class and/or small-group instruction using concrete manipulative objects, then pictorial representations, and finally abstract representations of simple algebraic equations.

Core Program: Algebra Readiness: https://www.sraonline.com

SRA Algebra Readiness teaches concepts introduced as early as Grade 2 through Algebra I to ensure that students are brought to mastery of pre-Algebra skills and concepts. SRA Algebra Readiness spirals development needed for success in an Algebra I program.

Core Math Program: Saxon Mathematics Program: www.harcourtachieve.com

Saxon Math, published by Harcourt Achieve, is a scripted curriculum that blends teacher-directed instruction of new material with daily distributed practice of previously learned concepts and procedures. Students hear the correct answers and are explicitly taught procedures and strategies. Other key factors of the program include frequent monitoring of student achievement and extensive daily routines that emphasize practice of number concepts and procedures and use of representations.

Core Math Program: Math Expressions: http://www.hmco.com/indexf.html

Math Expressions, published by Houghton Mifflin Company, blends student-centered and teacher-directed approaches. Students question and discuss mathematics, but are explicitly taught effective procedures. There is an emphasis on using multiple specified objects, drawings, and language to represent concepts, and an emphasis on learning through the use of real-world situations. Students are expected to explain and justify their solutions.

Solving Math Word Problems: Teaching Students With Learning Disabilities Using Schema-Based Instruction: www.proedinc.com

This intervention, developed by Dr. Asha Jitendra, is a teacher-directed program designed to teach critical word problem–solving skills to students with disabilities in the elementary and middle grades. The program is carefully designed to promote conceptual understanding using schema-based instruction (SBI) and provides the necessary scaffolding to support learners who struggle with math word problems.

Solve It! A Practical Approach to Teaching Mathematical Problem-Solving Skills: http://www.exinn.net/solve-it.html

Solve It! is a curriculum designed to improve the mathematical problem-solving skills of students in the upper elementary, middle, and secondary school grades—including students with disabilities who are having difficulties solving mathematical

(Continued)

(Continued)

problems. This program helps teachers help students develop the processes and strategies used by good problem solvers. Explicit instruction in mathematical problem solving is provided in lessons that teach critical cognitive and metacognitive processes. This research-based program is designed for easy inclusion in a standard mathematics curriculum. Solve It! was validated and refined in intervention studies with students with mathematical learning disabilities between 12 and 18 years of age.

Note: This list in not intended to be comprehensive, just a sample selection of programs and interventions to consider for use within your school's RTI math model.

Number Sense 5
and Initial
Math Skills

To achieve in mathematics, students must acquire a good sense of numbers early in their academic career. Without it, students may suffer in math for a long time. Geary, Hoard, and Hamson (1999) found that students with mathematics-based disabilities show difficulties with counting knowledge, number naming and writing, and memory retrieval as compared to their nondisabled peers as early as the first grade. Geary and his colleagues conjectured that these early difficulties in basic math would affect their future mathematics learning. The National Mathematics Advisory Panel (NMAP) (2008) argues that students must understand whole numbers and the operations with these whole numbers by Grade 4. This early sense of mathematics is called number sense (Dehaene, 1997; Gersten & Chard, 1999).

The National Council of Teachers of Mathematics (NCTM) (2000) defined number sense as "moving from the initial development of basic counting techniques to more sophisticated understanding of the size of numbers, number relationships, patterns, operations, and place value" (p. 79). Gersten and Chard (1999) clarified this broad term to mean "a child's fluidity and flexibility in using and manipulating numbers, an almost intuitive sense of what numbers mean, and an ability to perform mental mathematics and look at the world and make what, in essence, boils down to quantitative comparisons without difficulty" (p. 12).

With a strong sense of number, students are more capable to experience success in mathematics. The work of Jordan and her colleagues confirms this relationship. In a study of more than 200 kindergartners tracked to the end of the first grade, Jordan, Kaplan, Locuniak, and Ramineni (2007) found that number sense reliably predicts mathematics achievement. In fact, performance and development of number sense in kindergarten more accurately predicted first-grade mathematics performance than any other factor tested. Thus, all RTI math models must be prepared to intervene with number sense, particularly with young children who show early evidence of math difficulties. Without early intervention in number sense, students struggle and frustrations may extend well into elementary school, leading to difficulties in many other areas of math.

To explain the need for number sense, let's look at two students: one who understands place value, Caroline, and one who does not, Jason. For a problem like 32 + 13, Jason, who is still counting addition on his fingers, will have to count up from 32, thirteen times. However, Caroline, who understands place value but is still adding on her fingers, will add 3 tens + 1 ten and 2 ones + 3 ones. They both will conclude the answer is 45, but Caroline is quicker at obtaining the accurate solution and has a better grasp of base 10.

Demonstrating Number Sense With Addition

32	3 tens + 2 units
+ 13	+ 1 ten + 3 units
	4 tens + 5 units

In a subtraction problem with borrowing such as 43 − 15, Caroline's strength in place value will give her a profound advantage over Jason. While Jason will try to count out the difference between the two numbers or with a decent strategy count down from 43, Caroline will approach numbers by decomposing each number and organize the numbers based on their place value.

Demonstrating Number Sense With Subtraction

43	4 tens + 3 units	3 tens + 13 units
− 15	−1 ten − 5 units	− 1 ten − 5 units
		2 tens + 8 units = 28

In this example, neither student has a profound grasp of number sense (i.e., counting on fingers does not show strong number sense; Jordan, Kaplan, Ramineni, & Locuniak, 2008). However, Caroline's understanding of the place value component can lead to a more fluent problem-solving procedure. This chapter will focus on what to look for in assessing number sense and some possible interventions for teaching number sense.

ASSESSMENTS OF NUMBER SENSE

With such importance placed on number sense, it is important to implement a high-quality number sense assessment battery as early as kindergarten in order to determine who requires intervention. Additionally, Gersten, Clarke, and Jordan (2007) recommend using progress monitoring for number sense to track students longitudinally. Such progress monitoring works well within the framework of an RTI model. Number sense assessments should occur through at least the end of third grade and most preferably through fifth grade in order to help teachers adjust for student learning. Areas of number sense that should be tracked include but are not limited to the following:

1. Numeral recognition—identification and recall of numeral names (Figure 5.1) and corresponding quantity (Figure 5.2)

   > 2 means two which is counting 1, 2 things.

2. Magnitude comparison—accurate comparison of larger and smaller quantities based on concrete and pictorial representation of number and place value (Figure 5.3)

   > Circle which is larger: 14 or 41

3. Strategic counting—use of an efficient strategy of counting for single-digit addition and subtraction problems

4. Fact fluency or number combinations (discussed in Chapter 6)

   > Three larger than 9 is, 10, 11, 12. . . 12.

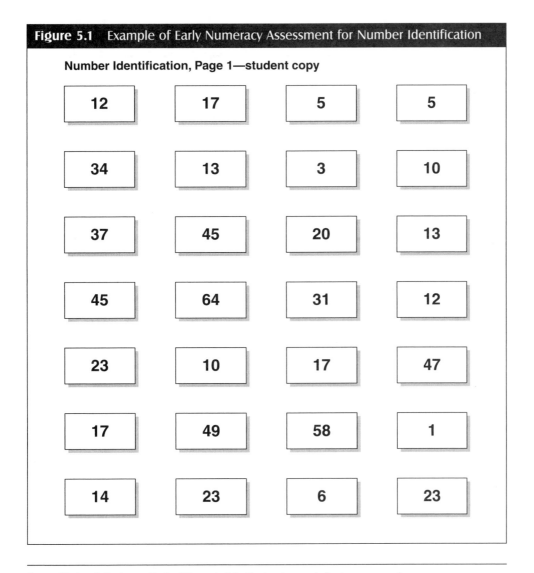

Figure 5.1 Example of Early Numeracy Assessment for Number Identification

Number Identification, Page 1—student copy

12	17	5	5
34	13	3	10
37	45	20	13
45	64	31	12
23	10	17	47
17	49	58	1
14	23	6	23

Source: National Center on Student Progress Monitoring (www.studentprogress.org).

Figure 5.2 Example of Early Assessment for Quantity Discrimination

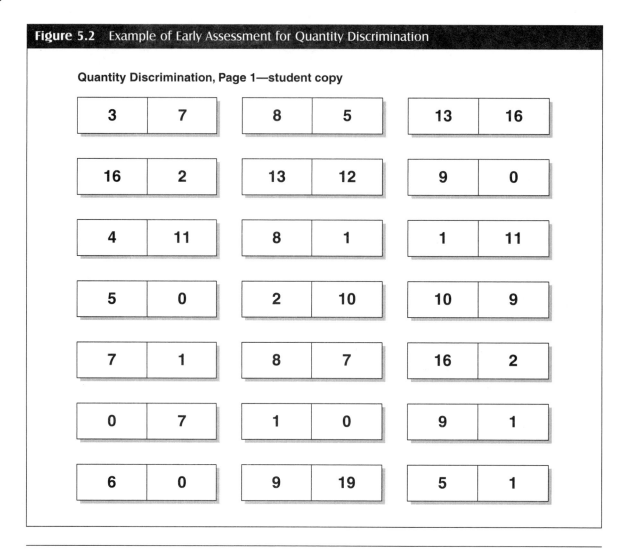

Quantity Discrimination, Page 1—student copy

Source: National Center on Student Progress Monitoring (www.studentprogress.org).

INSTRUCTIONAL DELIVERY OF NUMBER SENSE

Since assessment drives instruction and intervention, "high-quality core instruction in kindergarten and first and second grade is critical to prevent mathematics difficulties" (Bryant et al., 2008, p. 21). Although much of this chapter appears to push for curricular interventions, effective instruction should not be disregarded, particularly for early learners. The high-quality instruction should match the curricular needs of the students and any standards required. According to Bryant and his colleagues (2008), the core curriculum should include 11 components:

1. Clarity of objectives

2. A focus on teaching one skill at a time

3. Use of concrete and pictorial representations

Figure 5.3 Example of Early Assessment for Missing Number

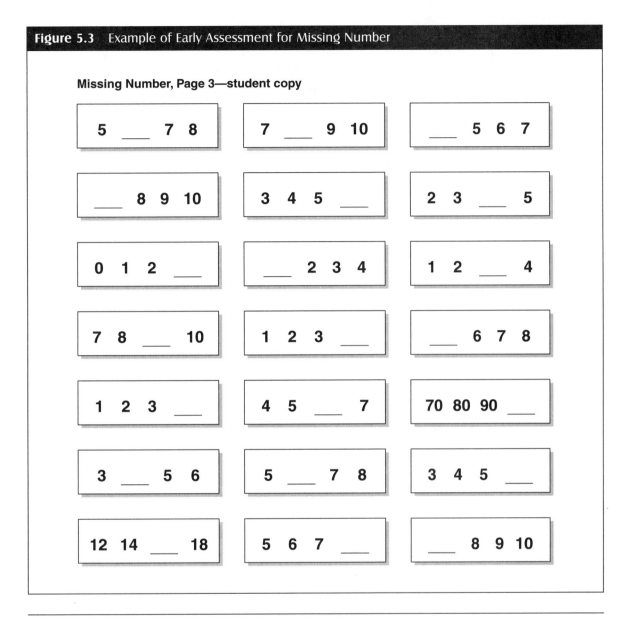

Missing Number, Page 3—student copy

5 ___ 7 8	7 ___ 9 10	___ 5 6 7
___ 8 9 10	3 4 5 ___	2 3 ___ 5
0 1 2 ___	___ 2 3 4	1 2 ___ 4
7 8 ___ 10	1 2 3 ___	___ 6 7 8
1 2 3 ___	4 5 ___ 7	70 80 90 ___
3 ___ 5 6	5 ___ 7 8	3 4 5 ___
12 14 ___ 18	5 6 7 ___	___ 8 9 10

Source: National Center on Student Progress Monitoring (www.studentprogress.org).

4. Explicit instruction

5. Adequately matched textbook examples to student problems

6. Adequate practice opportunities

7. Continuous review of prerequisite skills

8. Error pattern analysis and planned corrective feedback

9. Vocabulary that matches the objective taught in a comprehensible way

10. Explicitly taught problem-solving strategies

11. Progress monitoring

Each of these components can be included when teaching number sense (and a number of other math skills, for that matter). While most of these components have been discussed at least once already in this book, some have received less attention. That does not mean they are not important. For example, "adequately matched textbook examples to student problems" means matching what I model to what students have to answer. Some textbooks more accurately match problems than others. As a teacher, it is important to review the work samples and student assignment thoughtfully and in advance to assigning it. Additionally, textbook adoption committees need to review textbooks for such high-quality components as well.

In addition to well-designed problems in a textbook, the instruction should match the number sense needs of K–1 students and, for intervention, second-grade students who struggle. The design of the math textbook or program can have a negative or positive effect on student performance and must be considered when designing interventions. A math textbook or program that emphasizes Bryant and his colleagues' (2008) 11 instructional components is important to student success. Once a high-quality core instructional program is identified, it is important that it contains some key curricular elements that were instrumental in its selection for use.

CURRICULAR ELEMENTS OF A NUMBER SENSE INTERVENTION

The teacher is the ultimate factor in student performance. Effective teachers make continual adjustments and continually improve instruction. Ineffective teachers fail repeatedly in the same situations. However, the content that teachers teach is the purpose of each lesson and is expected to be remembered by the students. The curricular items listed below are some of the essential elements of number sense. A student's knowledge of number recognition, magnitude comparison, strategic counting principles, counting on and counting down, counting the difference, skip counting, place value, base ten, fact fluency, and number combinations all contribute to his number sense and thus contribute to his future success in mathematics. The rest of this chapter focuses on effective ways to deliver each of these elements so that the student can achieve success in mathematics.

Number Recognition

In order to help students learn their numbers and the corresponding quantity, it is important to start in a hands-on, concrete format. Start by saying the number and drawing it for them. Then, have the students say the number and draw it. To avoid motor and writing concerns, use a plate of shaving cream or a pan of rice, salt, or sand for the student to write the number. Starting at the top for each number, have students use their index finger to write the numeral. If students are slow to write it accurately, have another student make the numeral once and have the student who is struggling trace the written numeral. Also, use an auditory memorization tool to make the numeral. By using a "catchy" phrase or rhyme, students are more likely to memorize the shape of each numeral (Figure 5.4). Teach each number one at a time until the students show recognition and ability to draw it.

Figure 5.4   Fun Sayings to Help Students Write Digits

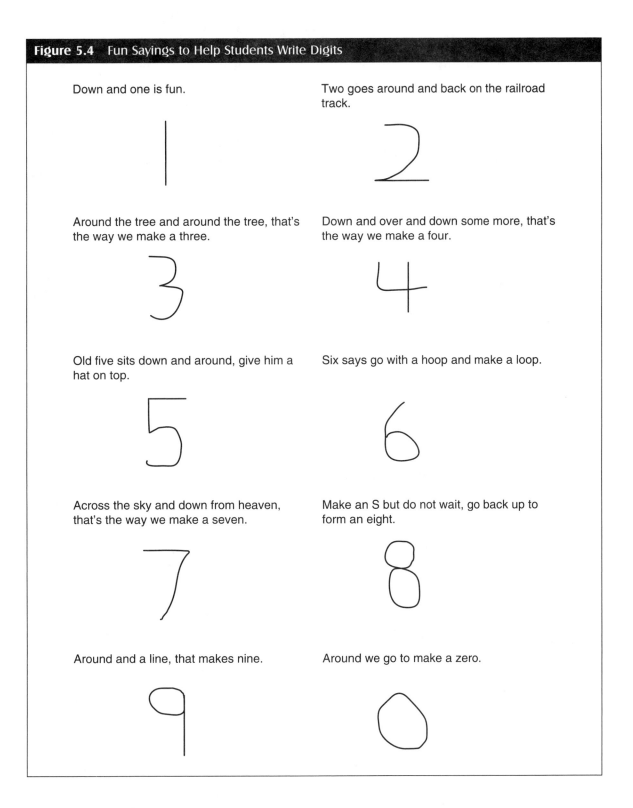

Down and one is fun.

Two goes around and back on the railroad track.

Around the tree and around the tree, that's the way we make a three.

Down and over and down some more, that's the way we make a four.

Old five sits down and around, give him a hat on top.

Six says go with a hoop and make a loop.

Across the sky and down from heaven, that's the way we make a seven.

Make an S but do not wait, go back up to form an eight.

Around and a line, that makes nine.

Around we go to make a zero.

When creating a quantity comparison to the numeral, there are a couple of possible approaches. One approach is to teach the connection by having students count objects that correspond to that numeral. Another approach is to have the students count up to that number. For example, when practicing a 6, students have to count to six when writing the numeral. A third approach is to use a dot notation approach. Strategically placed dots on the numeral help the student count to match the number quantity with the numeral. The work of James Hanrahan (see Simon & Hanrahan, 2004) has documented the effectiveness of using the dot format for teaching the quantity–numeral connection.

The dot pattern in Figure 5.5 shows a potential use of dot notation that depicts not only the number that may be counted, such as three dots for the number 3, but a different dot notation for a different place value. While most dot notation programs use the same notation for different place values, slight variance of place values will help with computation, for example, with double-digit computation. Carefully designed notation and representations can help prepare students for future math challenges, such as magnitude comparisons.

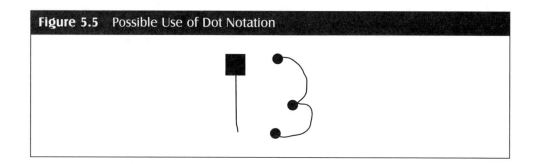

Figure 5.5   Possible Use of Dot Notation

Magnitude Comparison

When comparing the size or magnitude of two numerals, any of the three methods for learning quantity are useful. The most useful instructional tool for multidigit numbers is concrete objects. Have the students match the numeral with a set of concrete objects and then compare the sizes. Using objects that differentiate place value in a base 10 system helps build the place value understanding of the number. For example, when comparing 31 and 13, students must recognize that for 31, the 3 means 3 tens and the 1 means 1 unit or one. For 13, it means 1 ten and 3 ones. Placing size-relative objects next to each other more clearly shows the magnitude differences.

Figure 5.6 shows one method for magnitude comparisons. Using concrete objects that accurately represent base 10 quantities allows students to make correct assumptions and produce thoughtful answers in regard to determining and comparing quantities. In this example, the student is asked to indicate which quantity is greater. Using a gator mouth, the student is to open the gator mouth toward the larger quantity. The size-relative concrete objects allow the student to more accurately answer the question.

Figure 5.6 Helping Students Recognize Magnitudes of Numbers

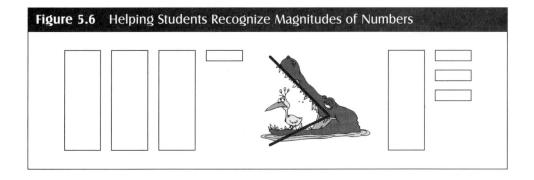

Once students grow successfully using concrete objects, teach students to draw pictorial depictions of those concrete objects. Finally, have the students mentally picture the size of the number for comparisons. While concrete objects and pictorial representations are important in development, they are meant to be methods of developing abstract, mental understanding.

Strategic Counting

Counting procedures help build accuracy in early computation and serve as important precursor skills in developing fluency (Bryant et al., 2008). There are several possible counting strategies to pull from when teaching early computation. Use concrete objects, like plastic bears, counter chips, or sticks, to show the counting strategies. Once students show some accuracy with the counting strategy, remove the objects and show the strategy on a number line. Eventually incorporate a multilevel number path, like an abacus, to support the base 10 concept. Also, it is important to teach students to recognize the computation sign and what that sign means.

Addition: Counting On

Start by teaching students to count from the first number when adding. As students grow more accurate with this approach, teach them the commutative property by starting with the larger number. For example, for 2 + 8, the student says, "Eight," and counts two more, "nine, ten." "2 + 8 equals 10." (See Figure 5.7.) The student may start by using his fingers to help recall the second number. This is not unacceptable, but it is important to encourage the student to mentally recall the second number when counting (Jordan et al., 2008).

Figure 5.7 Counting-On Strategy for 2 + 8

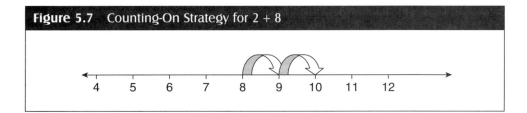

Subtraction: Counting Down

For subtraction, start by teaching students to start with the first number and then count down from that number according to the second number. For example, for 9 – 4, the student says, "Nine," and then counts down four more, "eight, seven, six, five." "9 – 4 equals 5." (See Figure 5.8.) Just like with addition, the student may need to use his fingers to keep track of the second number. Do not mark this as incorrect, but encourage him to try to remember the second number without using his fingers.

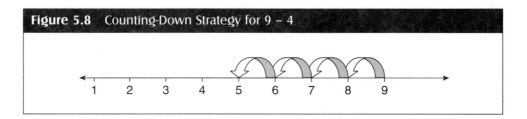

Figure 5.8   Counting-Down Strategy for 9 – 4

Subtraction: Counting the Difference

A more advanced counting strategy for "simple" subtraction is counting the difference between the numbers. If two numbers are close together on the number line, then this strategy is efficient. For example, for 14 – 11, the student starts with the lowest number, "eleven," and then counts up, "twelve (one), thirteen (two), fourteen (three)." "The difference between 14 and 11 is 3." (See Figure 5.9.)

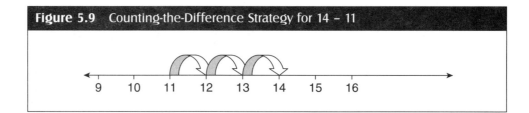

Figure 5.9   Counting-the-Difference Strategy for 14 – 11

Adding to Multiplication: Skip Counting

For building multiplication skill, teach skip counting, For example, for 5 × 3, the student says, "3, 6, 9, 12, 15." For 3 × 5, the student should say, "5, 10, 15." There are several ways to use music and songs to memorize skip counting. For example, teachers often use "Lou, Lou, Skip to My Lou" when teaching the 2s.

Skip count, skip count, count by 2s

Skip count, skip count, count by 2s

Skip count, skip count, count by 2s

We can count to 20.

2, 4, 6, 8, 10, 12, 14, 16, 18, 20.

Addition and Place Value: Plus 10

Using concrete objects followed by an abacus or hundreds chart allows the teacher to show how plus ten changes the tens place only. For example, $24 + 10$ makes the number 34 (see Table 5.1).

Table 5.1	Building Place Value Knowledge				
20	21	22	23	24	25
30	31	32	33	34	35

Note: This is a cut of a 100s chart.

Place Value: Equals 10

To further teach the base 10 system, teach combinations of numbers that equal 10. Showing a 10 frame or other base 10 graphic organizer, teach students to use a counting strategy to see what numbers equal 10. For example, $4 + ? = 10$. Using a base 10 graphic organizer, the student sees how this problem might be set up on a number line for future use. The student then can count, group, or recognize the quantity of open frames (marked with an O in the example) to determine that $4 + 6 = 10$ (see Table 5.2). Alternatively, some teachers prefer to use 10 frames to accomplish this lesson. A 10 frame is good because it matches the number of fingers per row in order to help create a match. However, it should also be used to prepare the student to use a base 10 graphic organizer and eventually a number line. Using either approach is a good stepping stone and one that can help introduce fact families and number combinations. For example, once a student learns that $4 + 6 = 10$, the student can use the same graphic organizer to learn that $6 + 4 = 10$, $10 - 4 = 6$, and $10 - 6 = 4$.

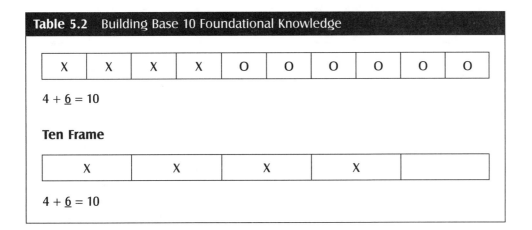

Table 5.2　Building Base 10 Foundational Knowledge

X	X	X	X	O	O	O	O	O	O

$4 + \underline{6} = 10$

Ten Frame

X	X	X	X	

$4 + \underline{6} = 10$

Fact Fluency or Number Combinations

Counting strategies are important for development of number sense and fact accuracy. However, students must not only be accurate, they must also be quick. Locuniak and Jordan (2008) found that kindergartners' number sense predicts second-grade calculation fluency. Thus, an efficient counting strategy that brings students from concrete to abstract thought processes can help in this regard. Although achieving fact fluency is promising, it is one of the most stubborn barriers to students' successes in later grades. Inefficient calculations and lack of fact fluency can hinder multiple-step problem solving (NMAP, 2008). Chapter 6 will outline how to improve students' fact fluency. One number sense preparatory step to fluent calculations is to decrease the number of facts to be memorized.

Teaching students combinations of numbers can help reduce the number of facts to be memorized. To a student, $7 + 3 = 10$ is a different problem than $3 + 7 = 10$. That is good, because they are different. However, an early introduction to the commutative property reveals that the sum of 7 and 3, no matter in what order they are presented, is 10. Teaching fact families is important when teaching basic facts. Learning the commutative, associative, and identity properties can help aid students to learn a larger quantity of computational facts and mathematical reasoning. Figure 5.10 shows a graphical way to portray those facts that should be practiced and recited.

Note: For fear of presenting another triangle in an RTI text, we turned it upside down.

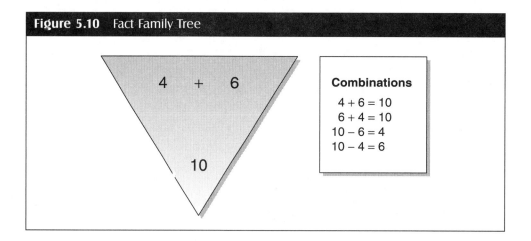

Figure 5.10   Fact Family Tree

$4 + 6$

10

Combinations

$4 + 6 = 10$
$6 + 4 = 10$
$10 - 6 = 4$
$10 - 4 = 6$

IN CONTEXT

Along with explicitly taught counting strategies and place value lessons, students need to see how math and numbers are used in their lives. Open your lessons with the use of everyday items, such as calendars, newspapers, and maps. For example, calendars use a multitude of bases from 7 for weeks to 28–31 for months. Thus, teaching base 10 competencies will not be easy to explain. However, calendar use can be used for counting on and counting down when planning events, such as birthdays and holidays. Additionally, grouping numbers of weeks can help introduce the concept of multiplication (e.g., 3 weeks × 7 days/week = 21 days).

Teach parents strategies to take home and use around the house, at the playground, and on the way to school. Math exists all around us. Schools conduct parent nights to bring families in and talk about their children's education. Along with talking about what *has* happened in school, a parent night can be used to talk about what *will* happen in school. Some of the content covered in mathematics is taught differently than when parents were in school. Additionally, some parents might not remember all the math concepts or procedures. A parent night can provide an opportunity to learn or relearn some of the mathematics. When possible, use students from previous years to come in and explain the upcoming math concepts to parents. This isn't designed to embarrass some parents but rather to encourage the how and why behind the mathematics being taught.

SUMMARY

The focus of this chapter was on teaching intervening with number sense to early-grade students who evidence early difficulties in math. Essential number sense curricular elements were described and instructional delivery and strategies were detailed using pictures and vignettes. The earlier students interact with the math in their environment, the more they can connect number sense to their lives. Also, the more fun they see in math, the better the motivation for continuing to learn it. Math is a complex subject. A strong start is important. A strong will is essential.

Building Students' **6** Proficiency With Whole Numbers

It is time for the debate regarding the importance of computation fluency and factual automaticity and time for math teachers to devote instructional time to teach computation fluency and automaticity of the basic facts.

—Paul J. Riccomini, 2009 (personal quote)

The debate over whether or not to teach basic facts and computation to proficiency is very similar to the argument in reading of whether or not to teach phonological and phonemic awareness. The field of reading has engaged in this discussion for many years and even currently continues to debate how much time and commitment must be spent on these reading components despite the rather larger research support for their importance to children's early literacy development and long-term reading outcomes. Given that the field of mathematics education is not as well researched as the reading field, the debate over what amount of emphasis computational proficiency and automaticity of basic facts should be afforded will continue for quite some time. This chapter will provide a brief overview of recommendations made by the National Mathematics Advisory Board (NMAP, 2008) regarding proficiency with whole numbers, and general guidelines for building proficiency with whole numbers. The chapter concludes with a brief description of two programs (Mastering Math Facts and PALS Math) that are designed to promote mathematical proficiency for students in Grades K–6.

IMPORTANCE OF PROFICIENCY IN WHOLE NUMBERS

No one really knows why some students fail to develop automaticity with the basic facts; however, we all know that students who do not develop automaticity will struggle as mathematics requirements become more complex. A profile of students who are struggling in mathematics generally includes problems with automatic recall of basic facts. Obviously, mathematics is much more than basic facts; however, basic facts are a necessary set of skills for students to have if they are to become mathematically proficient.

> "A focused, coherent progress of mathematics learning, with an emphasis on proficiency with key topics, should become the norm in elementary and middle school mathematics curricula."
>
> —*NMAP, 2008*

Proficiency is now the goal for all students. The NMAP (2008) defines proficiency as students who understand key concepts; achieve automaticity as appropriate; develop flexible, accurate, and automatic execution of standard algorithms; and use competencies to solve problems. Additionally, the panel provided an example along with the definition that spoke directly about basic facts. High school algebra teachers have experienced firsthand the ramifications of students who have failed to develop automaticity with basic facts; learning algebra becomes extremely difficult.

The NMAP (2008) surveyed more than 743 algebra teachers and reported a predominant view from these teachers that there should be a greater focus at elementary school level on proficiency of basic mathematics concepts and skills (p. 9). Mathematical programs are shifting away from focusing exclusively on concepts and problem solving and are targeting a more balanced approach. In a balanced approach, a mathematical program will develop proficiency with basic computational and procedural skills, promote conceptual understanding, and systematically move students toward being strategic problem solvers.

Although mathematical proficiency involves many aspects of mathematical knowledge (e.g., concepts, procedures, algorithms, vocabulary, problem solving, reading, motivation, computation), developing automaticity with basic facts should be the expectation of Tier 2 instruction at the elementary and middle grades. Gersten and his colleagues recommend at least 10 minutes devoted daily toward developing computational fluency (Gersten et al., 2009). Keeping with the recommendation from algebra teachers and more than 16,000 research studies reviewed, the NMAP (2008) articulated a set of proficiency benchmarks representing the most critical foundations for students to learn in their elementary and middle school mathematics program. Refer to Table 1.4 on p. 14 for the benchmarks. These critical benchmarks should have a major influence in the decision-making process of educators implementing RTI for elementary and middle grades. These benchmarks offer priorities that should be targeted at all instructional tiers when students are struggling.

GENERAL RECOMMENDATIONS FOR BUILDING PROFICIENCY

There are no secret recipes or magic math wands that can be used to help students develop proficiency and automaticity; rather, a systematic approach that maximizes instructional time provides students the most probability of developing automaticity. As RTI teams begin to address proficiency and automaticity, six recommendations should be considered: (1) specific criterion for introducing new facts, (2) intensive practice on newly introduced facts, (3) systematic practice of previously learned facts, (4) adequate instructional time, (5) progress monitoring and record keeping, and (6) motivational procedures (Stein, Kinder, Silbert, & Carnine, 2006).

Specific Criterion for Introducing New Facts

One plausible explanation for students' lack of proficiency is that the number of facts taught at one time or in a very short period of time can overwhelm their processing capacity (i.e., working memory). To help students who might have issues with memory, teachers can chunk problems into more manageable sizes. The reason why phone numbers are no more than 10 digits and grouped (i.e., chunked) into smaller sets is because it helps people remember the numbers; the same principle is applied to Social Security numbers (e.g., chunked into groups of 3-2-4). This "chunking" of information facilitates learning by providing students manageable pieces of information. When planning instruction to build proficiency or automaticity, consider how information can be chunked or grouped together in smaller parts for instruction and practice.

When students experience difficulties understanding the meaning or concept of a computational operation, using visual representations, such as the CRA sequence of instruction, has shown evidence of success, especially in computational facts (Maccini & Gagnon, 2000; Miller & Mercer, 1993). CRA requires an accurate representation of the most efficient problem-solving method per computational operation that helps the student develop from a concrete understanding to pictorial representation to abstract. The purpose of the concrete step is to build more accurate recall of the procedural steps to solving the problem. The pictorial representation and abstract steps help build faster solutions that follow the same steps as in the concrete step. Figure 6.1 shows the concrete steps to solving a subtraction of integers problem, $^{+}2 - {}^{-}4$. In this problem, the student is taught to reason the operation being asked in the number sentence (i.e., subtraction or addition of a negative). The purpose of these problem-solving steps is not to merely gain accuracy but to eventually build fluency of adding and subtracting integers. See Riccomini and Witzel (2009) for how to teach students to build proficiency with integer computation. Thus, like most of the examples in the previous chapter on number sense, these steps should be followed by practice that helps build fluency and automaticity.

Intensive Practice on Newly Introduced Facts

Practice combined with instruction is the best way to promote automaticity. Often teachers try to build automaticity with facts through the use of flash cards or "mad minutes." In doing these type of activities, students work their way through many facts as quickly as possible. It is effective for some children, but for others it does not build proficiency. One possible explanation is that in this type of practice format, students are actually practicing each individual fact only one time, even though the mad minutes may contain 60–100 facts. Effective intensive practice means students have multiple opportunities to practice the same fact;

Figure 6.1 Concrete Example of $^+2 - ^-4$

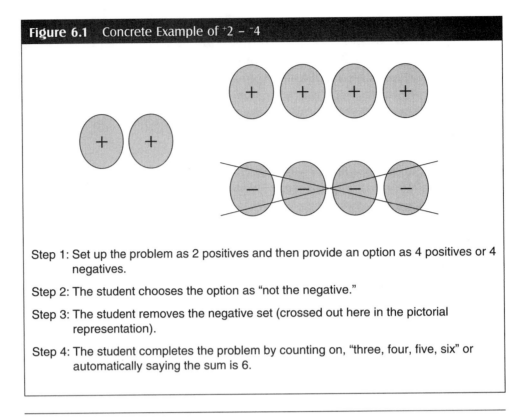

Step 1: Set up the problem as 2 positives and then provide an option as 4 positives or 4 negatives.

Step 2: The student chooses the option as "not the negative."

Step 3: The student removes the negative set (crossed out here in the pictorial representation).

Step 4: The student completes the problem by counting on, "three, four, five, six" or automatically saying the sum is 6.

Source: Adapted from Riccomini, P., & Witzel, B. (2009). *Computation of integers: Math interventions for elementary and middle grades students.* Upper Saddle River, NJ: Pearson Education Inc.

therefore, built-in repetition facilitates automaticity. On a cautionary note, intensive practice does not mean a worksheet with 100 problems that takes students 20 minutes to complete. Rather, intensive practice distributed across a period of time is an excellent way to build proficiency and automaticity, certainly a consideration in Tier 2 instructional supports.

Systematic Practice on Previously Introduced Facts

As students begin committing facts to automaticity and moving on to new facts, it is vital that the teacher provide systematic opportunities to practice previously learned facts. This systematic practice facilitates permanent retention. This is especially important for students with learning disabilities who generally demonstrate retention issues. Previously learned information does not have to be practiced as intensively as new information. As students progress through the sequence of math facts, previously learned facts are systematically faded from the practice activities. Tier 2 instruction time is a logical setting for which systematic practice opportunities are provided.

Adequate Instructional Time

Instructional time is at a premium in the school, especially with the heavy focus on reading and numerous standards at each grade level that teachers are responsible for teaching. It is important to maximize instructional time as much as possible. Building proficiency and automaticity should involve part of the allocated instructional time for mathematics. We have recommended that students receive a minimum of 50–60 minutes of instructional time devoted to math. As little as 5–7 minutes can be dedicated to instructional activities that facilitate automaticity of basic facts. Students should not spend the majority of math class doing practice worksheets. Proficiency in mathematics is much more than the automatic recall of basic facts, but the importance of automaticity with the basic facts should not be underestimated. Use instructional time wisely and efficiently.

Progress Monitoring and Record Keeping

Tracking students' growth and/or progress is also a critical aspect for building proficiency and automaticity. Graphing student progress on charts or tables provides teachers with instructional feedback. Additionally, students can use charts to set personal goals and increase motivation. Graphs and charts are also excellent tools for communication with parents. By graphing progress, students can take ownership of their learning and progress, which can become a motivating factor for many students.

Motivational Procedures

Motivation can play an important role in a child's education. Working with unmotivated students is identified as one of the most challenging aspects of teaching mathematics (NMAP, 2008). When students are not motivated, instruction can get bogged down and become difficult. The best way to motivate students is to make them feel successful. Sometimes teachers must start with small successes and work up toward larger successes. Teachers are masterful at providing students motivation for learning.

These general guidelines for building automaticity with basic facts are important considerations when designing instructional activities targeting automaticity. As a result of the renewed emphasis on automaticity, teachers are looking for programs that focus on building automaticity. There are many programs available and far too many to include in this chapter; however, a description of one program, Mastering Math Facts, is included because it is designed to follow the general guidelines discussed above.

BUILDING AUTOMATIC RECALL OF BASIC FACTS WITH THE MASTERING MATH FACTS PROGRAM

Mastering Math Facts is a structured program used to improve fluency and automaticity of the four basic mathematics operations: addition, subtraction, multiplication, and division (Crawford, 2003). The program specifically targets students in the elementary and middle school grades, but could also be used for students in high school. The program allows for a variety of practice structures including paired practice, whole-group practice, small-group practice, and/or individual practice. General procedures for using the program are described.

Mastering Math Facts Overview

Mastering Math Facts is a student-paced program designed to supplement the core mathematics program and focuses exclusively on automaticity of basic facts. Practice activities range from 5–10 minutes and can be delivered five days a week. The program is designed for students who are able to accurately compute single-digit computation facts (e.g., $3 \times 4 = 12$). It does not matter if students are still using a strategy (e.g., counting on, number line); as long as they are accurate, the program is appropriate (Crawford, 2003). The manual includes a detailed implementation guide, explicit teacher directions, goal sheets and goal-setting parameters, placement tests and progress-monitoring assessments, and student practice sheets and keys. The manual also includes certificates for positive reinforcement and sample parent letters explaining the program. Figure 6.2 includes an adapted student practice sheet from the program.

The program is implemented in three main stages (Crawford, 2003). First, teachers determine how quickly students can write by having them write as many numbers as they can in 1 minute. This is the initial basis for determining a student's goal. The program provides a goal sheet that allows teachers to quickly and easily set appropriate goals. Once goals are set, teachers can start all students on the same set of facts (e.g., Set A) or use a placement test to determine which set each student will start. Regardless of how the program is started, students can progress at their own rate. The next stage is for teachers and students to establish a routine or consistent structure for the practice activities. Each student is given a folder containing a practice sheet (see Figure 6.2), corresponding answer key, and progress-monitoring chart. Students can work in paired partners or small groups depending on the teacher's preference and student characteristics. Each student has 1 minute to correctly say as many facts as possible. Note that the student is not just saying the answer; the student is saying the entire fact. For example, if the fact is 9×8; the student will say "9 times 8 is 72." The connection students build by saying the entire fact is important to building automaticity.

Then, students have an additional minute to try to correctly say more than they did in the first attempt; partners exchange roles and repeat. Then, each student has 1 minute to correctly write as many facts as possible in an effort to beat their goal. Once students surpass the goal, they are recognized with some positive reinforcement and move on to the next set. Students who do not exceed their goal continue to practice on the same set until they are able to exceed their goal. The progression allows students ample time to commit small sets of facts to memory and systematically moves them through the sequence.

The final stage is for teachers to routinely administer 2-minute assessments at specified intervals. These 2-minute assessments serve to gauge overall progress. Students are responsible for correcting each other's 2-minute assessments and chart their own scores. Students are directed to try to exceed the score from the last 2-minute time assessment, and those who do are recognized (e.g., certificates included in program). Again, a student plotting his or her own progress builds a sense of ownership in one's learning.

The strength and effectiveness of this program lie in the instructional design features used throughout the practice lessons (Stein et al., 2006). First, facts are chunked into manageable groups so students are not overwhelmed. Second, the student practice sheets are designed to facilitate more frequent

---

Figure 6.2 Example Student Practice and Timed Test Worksheet From Mastering Math Facts

Set   Student practice sheet includes all facts learned up to this set.

9×7 4×4 8×9 3×9 4×4 9×8 7×9 4×4 5×2 9×7

9×7 2×8 8×9 3×9 4×4 9×8

Practice sheet contains 40 facts with the majority of facts coming from the new set.

1. The top is designed for a variety of practice formats:
   - Partner practice
   - Whole-group/small-group teacher-led practice
   - Individual practice
   - Written or oral practice
2. Specific correction procedures for students.
3. Practice is timed (2–3 minutes).
4. Students are trained on how to practice and that practice is monitored closely by the teacher.
5. Once practice is completed, students move to bottom half.

One-Minute Timing of Facts up to This Set

5×2 2×7 4×4 2×3 5×5 9×7 7×2 2×9 1×7 3×1

3×3 5×1 3×3 9×2 8×8

The timed test section contains 40 problems that include only facts that have been learned up to and including the new set.

Students have 1 minute to write as many correct facts as they can. When the 1 minute is up, students score their answers and check to see if they meet their goal.

If they did exceed their goal, they move on to the next set. If not, they continue to practice the current set.

Student Goal   Student Score

Source: Adapted from D. B. Crawford. (2003). *Mastering math facts: Blackline masters and answer keys.* Eau Claire, WI: Otter Creek Institute.

practice of the new facts, but also continue to provide practice on the facts from the previously learned sets, thereby increasing the number of opportunities on the new facts but still providing a cumulative review on previously learned facts. Third, the program has structured correction procedures that students follow during partner practice.

Students are not permitted to guess after missing a fact, but rather are stopped, told the correct answer, repeat the correct answer, and then go back three facts and start again. This method of correcting students is very effective because it does not allow guessing, which can lead to more confusion. Fourth, the program includes specific criteria for introducing new sets of facts. Students should not move on to the next set until exceeding their goal. Fifth, the program is intrinsically motivating to many students because they are competing against themselves and find it very rewarding when they are able to exceed their own goals.

The Mastering Math Program is a sequential approach to practicing math facts that promotes automatic recall and essential fundamental math skills needed for students to be successful in upper-level math courses (e.g., algebra and geometry). Students who are not automatic with basic facts are likely to struggle significantly as mathematics courses become more complex. This program can fill a major gap in many commercially available mathematics core programs by providing sufficient practice activities devoted to automatic recall of basic facts. This program or similar programs should be considered for use in your school's RTI model.

BUILDING PROFICIENCY WITH WHOLE NUMBERS THROUGH PALS MATH

Peer-assisted learning strategies in math (PALS Math) are evidenced-based instructional practices used to improve achievement and attitudes toward mathematics among diverse students in Grades K–6. During PALS Math, students work together to practice important foundation mathematics skills. General procedures for conducting PALS Math are described.

PALS Math Overview

PALS Math is a 16–18-week program designed to supplement the core mathematics program. Lessons range from 20–30 minutes and are delivered either twice a week or three times a week. There are three PALS Math programs available for kindergarten, Grade 1, and Grades 2–6. The PALS Math manual includes scripts to guide teachers through each lesson, all student materials needed for the 16 weeks of instruction, and a scope and sequence of mathematics concepts and skills covered. Table 6.1 provides an overview of mathematics concepts and skills covered in each grade level. Students spend the majority of the instructional time working with peers using a reciprocal teaching process, thus allowing all students ample opportunities to engage in mathematics tasks.

Table 6.1	Overview of Mathematics Concepts and Skills Covered in PALS Math, Kindergarten and Grade 1
PALS Math Program	*Mathematics Concepts and Skills Covered*
Kindergarten	**Number Concepts** • Recognizing numbers • Understanding or illustrating numbers • Writing numbers **Comparing Numbers** • Which is more? • Which is less? • More and less with spinner and number line **Addition and Subtraction Concepts**
Grade 1	**Number Concepts** **Comparing Numbers** **Addition and Subtraction** • One-digit +, – • Two-digit +, – **Place Value** **Missing Addends**

Source: From Fuchs, L. S., Fuchs, D., Yazdian, L., Powell, S., & Karns, K. (n.d.). *Peer-assisted learning strategies: Kindergarten math: Teacher manual.* Available for purchase from Peer-Assisted Learning Strategies Web site: http://www.kc.vanderbilt.edu/kennedy/pals; and Fuchs, L. S., Fuchs, D., Yazdian, L., Powell, S., & Karns, K. (n.d.). *Peer-assisted learning strategies: First-grade math: Teacher manual.* Available for purchase from Peer-Assisted Learning Strategies Web site: http://www.kc.vanderbilt.edu/kennedy/pals.

PALS Math is an evidence-based instructional methodology that teachers can use to promote important mathematics skills among students in elementary grades. The procedures used in PALS Math are based on 10+ years of experimental studies completed in various school settings, including Title I and non–Title I schools in both urban and suburban communities (Phillips, Fuchs, & Fuchs, 1994). In addition to improving the mathematics achievement of students with disabilities, other low-performing students as well as average-achieving students can benefit from PALS procedures.

PALS Math procedures capitalize on the use of peers as tutors to provide frequent verbal interactions and feedback on student mathematics performance. Through a series of structured activities, student pairs work together to complete a series of foundational mathematics tasks that improve computation skills (Calhoon & Fuchs, 2003), math readiness (Fuchs et al., 2001), and overall interest in math (Calhoon & Fuchs, 2003). Several benefits from PALS Math procedures are achieved including more time engaged in essential mathematics tasks, opportunities for success for all students, increases in mathematics achievement, improvement of students' attitude toward mathematics, improved social interactions, and applicability of implementation.

PALS Math is a classwide peer tutoring program that provides additional practice on important foundational mathematics skills. A PALS Math manual (Fuchs, Fuchs, Yazdian, Powell, & Karns, n.d.) provides an overview of the strategies and scripted lessons teachers can use when teaching. Additionally, materials needed to conduct the lessons (e.g., transparencies for instruction, signs for posting teams and pairings, point sheets, and prompt cards) are included in the manual.

Each PALS Math session involves students working together as coaches or players and taking turns completing various mathematics tasks for those particular lessons. Teachers pair students using a systematic ranking system and pairs change frequently. Teachers also select the skills-specific students who require additional practice. PALS Math activities typically are scheduled during time allocated for mathematics instruction; however, these procedures are primarily practice activities and should occur only after students have received teacher-directed instruction in the core mathematics program. Additionally, PALS Math is designed for all students; therefore, PALS Math is not scheduled when some students are out of the classroom for other activities (e.g., resource or speech).

PALS Math utilizes a competitive team approach. The teacher pairs every student in the class by placing a stronger math-performing student with a weaker math-performing student. Based on their overall mathematics performance, students are ranked from highest to lowest. Once teams are formed, partners work together to earn "smiley faces" for their teams based on accuracy on the mathematical tasks as well as for following rules, working cooperatively, and displaying appropriate coach and player behaviors. Each student has the opportunity to function as both a coach and a player for each PALS Math activity. Working with a partner also provides benefits for students struggling because of the immediate corrective feedback received and builds their mathematical confidence; these are especially important aspects for students who have struggled in the past.

PALS Math is a program that systematically provides all students additional structured practice opportunities on essential and fundamental computational skills required for mathematical proficiency. The combination of working with partners and the reward system also promotes positive social interactions and motivation for doing mathematics activities. PALS Math programs should be considered for implementation in schools' RTI math models.

SUMMARY

It is time for the debate regarding proficiency with whole-number computation and basic facts to end and time for teachers to devote instructional time to computational proficiency and automaticity of basic facts. Until the mathematics profile of struggling students and students with disabilities changes and no longer includes computational deficits and lack of automaticity with basic facts, it is an area that needs to be addressed instructionally. It would better serve students' needs if these types of practice activities that build automaticity and proficiency (Mastering Math Facts and PALS Math) were standard practice in the general education math class (Tier 1), but they are an essential part of Tier 2 instructional supports for students lacking in these areas.

Fractions and Decimals 7

Fractions and decimals have long eluded students, not just students with pervasive learning difficulties or learning disabilities, but also students who are average performing. With a goal of students preparing for and succeeding in algebra, the National Mathematics Advisory Panel (NMAP, 2008) concluded that students' difficulties with fractions are one of the largest obstacles for schools. Because of the continuous and widespread difficulty with fractions and decimals, RTI models must account for this potential trouble spot.

The usefulness of fractions and decimals in life is not a mystery. Most numbers used in work, personal finances, and even play are not whole numbers, but rather fractions or decimals. From tax payments, to credit card rates, to stock numbers, a citizen's inability to understand and work with fractions will greatly impair their financial freedom and empowerment. Therefore, the reasons for teaching fractions and decimals in school are self-explanatory.

Based on an understanding of division, a fraction is when a number is divided into equal parts. A fraction can be used to represent a part of a whole, a point on a number line, or a ratio between two numbers. Understanding fractions leads to working with graphs, to coefficients, and measurement and trigonometry. Fractions need to be taught early and effectively. Thus, RTI models must prepare interventions designed to help students who struggle early with fractions and decimals. Without effective interventions with fractions, a seemingly small problem can become a much larger and more invasive issue.

Many students at the secondary level understand little about how decimals are related to fractions other than that special key on their graphing

> "The curriculum should allow for sufficient time to ensure acquisition of conceptual and procedural knowledge of fractions (including decimals and percent) and of proportional reasoning. The curriculum should include representational supports that have been shown to be effective, such as number line representations, and should encompass instruction in tasks that tap the full gamut of conceptual and procedural knowledge, including ordering fractions on a number line, judging equivalence and relative magnitudes of fractions with unlike numerators and denominators, and solving problems involving ratios and proportion. The curriculum also should make explicit connections between intuitive understanding and formal problem solving involving fractions."
>
> —NMAP, 2008, p. 29

calculator. Using the Algebra Readiness Test, Sanders, Riccomini, and Witzel (2005) found that the two areas that high school algebra students with and without identified mathematics difficulties struggled with the most were decimals and fractions. In fact, these students' errors were so great that they were actually unprepared for their algebra course. As educators and interventionists, we must concentrate our efforts on fractions and decimals. We must show students what fractions and decimals are and how to compute them.

FRACTIONS IN THE STANDARDS

Fractions are so omnipresent in math concepts that they appear throughout a student's academic curriculum. The National Council of Teachers of Mathematics (NCTM, 2000) states that students in Grades 3–5 should understand the concept of fractions, how to find equivalent forms of fractions, and the addition and subtraction of fractions. In Grades 6–8, students should learn how to manipulate fractions in many math contexts. Among the listing for standards with fractions are the following (NCTM, 2000):

- Work flexibly with fractions, decimals, and percents to solve problems.
- Compare and order fractions, decimals, and percents efficiently and find their approximate locations on a number line.
- Understand the meaning and effects of arithmetic operations with fractions, decimals, and integers.
- Use the associative and commutative properties of addition and multiplication and the distributive property of multiplication over addition to simplify computations with integers, fractions, and decimals.
- Select appropriate methods and tools for computing with fractions and decimals from among mental computation, estimation, calculators or computers, and paper and pencil, depending on the situation, and apply the selected methods.
- Develop and analyze algorithms for computing with fractions, decimals, and integers and develop fluency in their use.
- Develop and use strategies to estimate the results of rational-number computations and judge the reasonableness of the results.
- Develop, analyze, and explain methods for solving problems involving proportions, such as scaling and finding equivalent ratios.

To further the NCTM's (2006) emphasis on fractions, the focal points for kindergarten through eighth grade stressed the need for students to become fluent with the computation of fractions. The NMAP (2008) added to the NCTM's emphasis by stating grade-level student expectations that show that understanding the concept of a fraction is only part of learning about fractions (see Table 7.1). Students should develop fluency with the computation of positive and negative fractions and apply that computation to more complex problems.

Table 7.1 National Mathematics Advisory Panel Benchmarks for Fractions	
Benchmark	*Description*
Fluency With Fractions	• By the end of Grade 4, students should be able to identify and represent fractions and decimals, and compare them on a number line or with other common representations of fractions and decimals.
	• By the end of Grade 5, students should be proficient with comparing fractions and decimals and common percent, and with the addition and subtraction of fractions and decimals.
	• By the end of Grade 6, students should be proficient with multiplication and division of fractions and decimals.
	• By the end of Grade 6, students should be proficient with all operations involving positive and negative integers.
	• By the end of Grade 7, students should be proficient with all operations involving positive and negative fractions.
	• By the end of Grade 7, students should be able to solve problems involving percent, ratio, and rate and extend this work to proportionality.

Source: From U.S. Department of Education, *Foundations for success: The final report of the National Mathematics Advisory Panel,* March 2008. Retrieved April 1, 2008, from http://www.ed.gov/about/bdscomm/list/mathpanel/report/final-report.pdf.

For a classroom teacher, Dr. Jim Milgrams reported to the NMAP in 2006 a more strict computational set of expectations per grade level and when to include the connection to decimals. The report listed the following:

Grade 3: Teach fractions, equivalent fractions.

Grade 4: Teach fluency with multiplication and decimals as well as the connection between fractions and decimals.

Grade 5: Teach students to become fluent with whole number division and to become fluent with addition and subtraction of fractions.

Grade 6: Teach fluency of multiplication and division of fractions and decimals, and show the connection between ratio and rate to whole number multiplication and division.

Grade 7: Teach students to understand and apply proportionality and similarity.

ASSESSMENT FOR FRACTIONS AND DECIMALS

There is a lack of assessment options available specific to fractions. Because of this limitation, many of the research reports that address fractions, decimals, and percents use teacher- or researcher-made assessments rather than a commercial assessment battery. For example, the National Library of Virtual Manipulatives includes a quick assessment for fractions (see http://enlvm.usu .edu/ma/classes/__shared/emready@fraction_concepts/info/fractions_rubric .pdf; also see Table 7.2).

Table 7.2 National Library of Virtual Manipulatives Assessment for Fractions		
Fraction Concepts Online Assessment Scoring Rubric		
Questions/Answers	*Score*	
1. What are fractions?		
• Things that tell you part of a whole	1	2, if both definition and example used
• Example	1	
• Other:		
2. What does the numerator (top number) describe?		
• How many you have	1	
• A piece of the whole	1	
• Other:		
3. What does the denominator (bottom number) describe?		
• How many make up a whole thing	1	
• The whole	1	
• Other:		
4. Write the fraction 5/8 using words.		
• Five eighths	1	
• Five out of eight	1	
• Other:		
5. Give 3 examples of fractions from the world around you.		
• Food related (shopping, cooking, ...) When we cook.	1	one point for every example up to 3
• Measurement/building related (ruler, measuring cup)	1	
• Getting gas	1	
• Talking about money	1	
• Other:		
6a. How many triangles does it take to cover the yellow shape?		
• 6	1	
• Other:	0	

Questions/Answers	Score
6b. One green triangle is __ out of __ triangles needed . . .	
• 1 out of 6	1
• 1 out of (answer from part a)	1
6c. Write the fraction using numbers.	
• 1/6	1
• 1/(answer from part a)	1
7. Which picture represents the fraction in the sentence below? I attend school 5 out of the 7 days in a week.	
• First pie, showing 5/7	1
• Other:	0
8. Which fraction is bigger? 7/10 and 6/10	
• 7/10	1
• Other:	0
9. Which fraction is larger? 2/3 and 5/9	
• 2/3	1
• Other:	0
10. Which fraction is larger? 4/6 and 2/3	
• They are the same	1
• Other:	0

Source: National Library of Virtual Manipulatives. Retrieved January 26, 2009, from http://nlvm.usu.edu/en/nav/siteinfo.html. Reprinted with permission.

In their assessment, they address defining a fraction, differentiating numerator and denominator, labeling fractions, and comparing the magnitude of two fractions. Witzel and Riccomini (2009) wrote a fractions intervention designed for middle school students. In their assessment, they include division with fractions in the answers, multiplication of fractions, division of fractions, finding equivalent fractions, simplifying fractions, and adding and subtracting fractions with like and unlike denominators. Although this assessment focused on the computation of fractions, when working with students in early to mid-elementary school, it is important to also address conceptual and vocabulary parts of fractions. We suggest assessing students' conceptual understanding of parts of a whole first, followed by vocabulary lessons for the meaning of numerator and denominator. Finally, assess the placement of the fraction along a number line. Computationally, first assess division with fractional answers then computation with fractions. Finally, assess students' solutions and problem solving of equivalent and simplified fractions. For extension of fractions ideas, incorporate fractions in other mathematical areas to see how the student adapts his or her problem solving to meet the computational and conceptual needs in the problem.

The lack of assessments with decimals is equally as dearth as with fractions. We suggest assessing decimals by their placement on a number line. Then, test students' place value knowledge of decimals. Next, assess simple computation with fractions. Do not bother with large and complex computation problems with decimals because the student's answer may be confounded with other concerns such as computational accuracy, fluency, and even number alignment.

WHEN ARE CALCULATORS SUFFICIENT?

Many students turn to calculators when they see decimals and fractions. While accurate calculations are highly important, it is also important that students understand what they are calculating and why they are performing certain steps during calculation. Teach the concepts and procedural calculations of fractions and decimals before allowing calculators to infiltrate the classroom problem solving. As a matter of fact, algebra teachers reported calculator dependence by students as a major problem for teaching algebra (NMAP, 2008).

Voices From the Field: What Algebra Teachers Say

To understand the experiences of Algebra teachers in the classroom, the National Math Panel commissioned a national survey of randomly chosen Algebra I teachers designed to elicit their views on student preparation, work-related attitudes and challenges, and use of instructional materials. The National Opinion Research Center at The University of Chicago conducted the survey in the spring and summer of 2007. Of the 310 public schools identified, 258 agreed to participate, and 743 teachers— a 72% response rate—completed the questionnaire.

The survey revealed that teachers rate their students' background preparation for Algebra I as weak. The three areas in which teachers report their students to have the poorest preparation are rational numbers, word problems, and study habits. When asked to provide a brief description of any changes they would like to see in the curriculum leading up to Algebra I, teachers most often cited the need for a greater focus at the elementary school level on proficiency with basic mathematical concepts and skills.

Sample responses representing this predominant view include:

- "Students need to be better prepared in basic math skills and not be quite so calculator dependent. Also, more training in thinking skills."
- "Make sure the 1st–8th grade teachers teach the foundations of math and that the students know their basic skills."
- "More focus on basics—students should already know order of operations, positive vs. negative numbers, fractions and decimals."

With regard to instructional materials, teachers, for the most part, do not regularly use technological tools. On average, teachers said they use these tools less than once a week. Low levels of computer use do not appear to be a reflection of insufficient access. About one-third of teachers never use the graphing calculator, and manipulative materials are used only occasionally.

In response to 10 options describing the challenges they face, a majority of the teachers (62%) rated "working with unmotivated students" as the "single most challenging aspect of teaching Algebra I successfully." Their second highest-rated challenge—11%—was making mathematics accessible and comprehensible. However, the written-in responses most frequently mentioned handling different skill levels in a single classroom. A substantial number of teachers consider mixed-ability groupings to be a "moderate" (30%) or "serious" (23%) problem, an item with a combined rating of 53% for "moderate" and "serious," second only to the combined rating of 64% for "too little parent/family support."

The survey results reinforce the research findings presented in the report, particularly the need to strengthen students' proficiency with rational numbers. Further, the Panel suggests that greater attention be focused on ways in which negative attitudes toward mathematics develop and how to overcome students' lack of motivation.

A full report on the survey is available (National Mathematics Advisory Panel, 2008).

The Panel wishes to express its appreciation to the teachers who participated in the survey. Their voices and experience proved valuable to the Panel's work.

Source: From U.S. Department of Education, *Foundations for success: The final report of the National Mathematics Advisory Panel,* March 2008. Retrieved April 1, 2008, from http://www.ed.gov/about/bdscomm/list/mathpanel/report/final-report.pdf.

The verbiage of the standard leads to the possible use of calculators. If a standard calls for understanding, approximating, determining, or using a certain algorithm or procedure, then the calculator is not necessarily purposeful. In fact, it might be counterproductive to the standard if students are to learn formulas or algorithms. If the standard is on accurate calculation, then the use of the calculator is acceptable. However, if the standard calls for calculation fluency and proficiency, then the calculator is unacceptable.

TEACHING THE "WHAT" WITH FRACTIONS AND DECIMALS

Fractions

1. Teach students to represent fractions and to label the parts of the fraction. For this conceptual representation, students fold a strip of paper (appropriately called a fraction strip) in a number of equal parts, four in this example. Darken the line along each fold. Ask students if each fold is equally sized. If the students agree they are all of equal size, then explain and label the four sections as the denominator. Then have them shade in a certain number of the sections and call them the numerator. Display the fraction that they just made and explain the parts. Then

have the students create more fraction strips followed by other physical representations of fractions. In the example below (Figure 7.1), students compare the fractions ½ and ¾ to find they do not equal the same overall quantity.

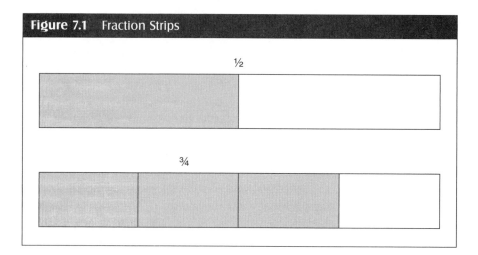

Figure 7.1 Fraction Strips

2. Show students how to identify the magnitude of fractions. Use the CRA sequence of instruction to help students develop this concept. If you started with fraction strips, then compare student-made fraction strips to pre-created ones for 0, ¼, ½, ¾, and 1. When you include more fraction strips of other denominators, show students how to order them from least to greatest. In the figure below (Figure 7.2), a student placed two fraction strips in order from least to greatest according to a number line.

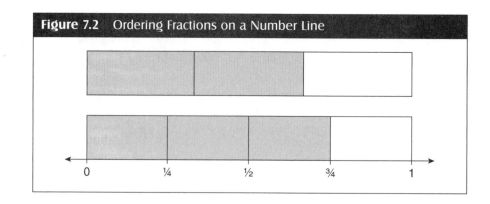

Figure 7.2 Ordering Fractions on a Number Line

Once students perform well with fractions between 0 and 1, expand the students' concept of fraction to mixed fractions such as 1⅓. Instead of using fraction strips, expand students' thinking to a point on a number line that represents a quantity. In Figure 7.3, one student placed a point on a number line to show where he thought 1⅓ fits.

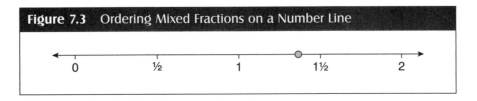

Figure 7.3 Ordering Mixed Fractions on a Number Line

3. Teach students to identify fractions with physical items such as pattern blocks (see Figure 7.4). Use one of the blocks to represent 1 whole. Then, have the students estimate by visual inspection the fraction that is represented by other shapes. Some students may need to create the same shape with the objects either beside the shape representing 1 whole or even on top of the shape representing 1 whole. Change the activity by showing which shape or group of shapes represents 1 whole.

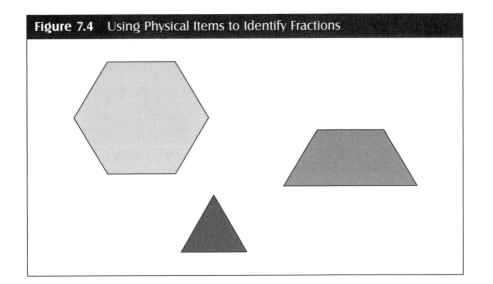

Figure 7.4 Using Physical Items to Identify Fractions

Decimals

1. Show students how to identify the magnitude of decimals. Have students identify the place value of indicators on the given number line and then identify where teacher-provided decimals fit on the line. Since this is an estimation activity, assess student performance according to where students place points and precisely where between indicators points were placed. In Figure 7.5, a student marked where he thinks 1.20 is on a number line.

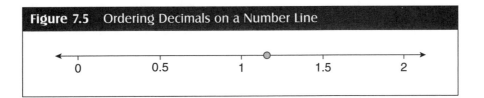

Figure 7.5 Ordering Decimals on a Number Line

2. Use graphic organizers to teach place value of decimals (see Table 7.3).

Table 7.3	Using Graphic Organizers to Represent Place Value			
Units	*Tenths*	*Hundredths*	*Thousandths*	*Ten-thousandths*
1	5	2	6	

Graphic organizers can be used to organize students' writing of decimals. To help practice this activity, have cards that list the decimal in abstract form. One student in a pair pulls the card and reads it to the other without revealing what it looks like on the card itself. On the board, the other student writes down what they hear (see Figure 7.6).

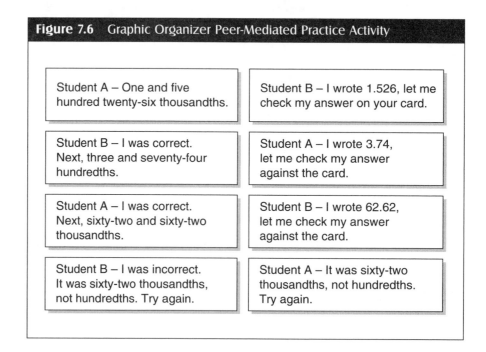

Figure 7.6 Graphic Organizer Peer-Mediated Practice Activity

Student A – One and five hundred twenty-six thousandths.

Student B – I wrote 1.526, let me check my answer on your card.

Student B – I was correct. Next, three and seventy-four hundredths.

Student A – I wrote 3.74, let me check my answer against the card.

Student A – I was correct. Next, sixty-two and sixty-two thousandths.

Student B – I wrote 62.62, let me check my answer against the card.

Student B – I was incorrect. It was sixty-two thousandths, not hundredths. Try again.

Student A – It was sixty-two thousandths, not hundredths. Try again.

Use class opportunities for students to interact with decimal place values. One way is through the "race to one" game with two dice (see Figure 7.7). Each role of a die represents one-hundredth. Two students take turns rolling the dice and exchanging ten-hundredths for one-tenth until one person finally makes it to one or larger. Each column uses different-colored tiles to represent one in that place value. This activity encourages decimal place value naming and illustrates exchanges that occur with addition of decimals.

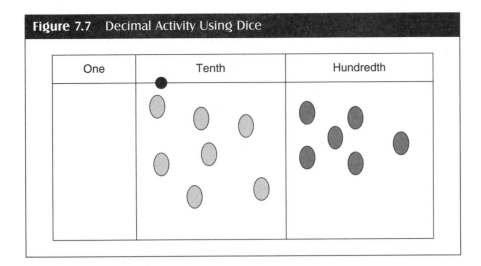

Figure 7.7 Decimal Activity Using Dice

3. If students need more physical representations of decimals, use base 10 blocks that are sized relative to their place value. This physical representation also lends itself to the concrete-representational-abstract sequence of instruction (CRA), which has shown a great benefit to students with mathematics difficulties, even with fractions (Butler, Miller, Crehan, Babbitt, & Pierce, 2003). So that students can re-create the physical form of the manipulative, avoid three objects that are differentiated by a three-dimensional attribute. For example, using base value blocks, do not use a cube and a flat square together unless the students are able to draw a differentiated form of each. In the example below (Figure 7.8), the square represents 1 unit, the long strips each represent one-tenth, and the small units each represent one-hundredth. In this example, the decimal 1.36, or one and thirty-six hundredths, is to be represented.

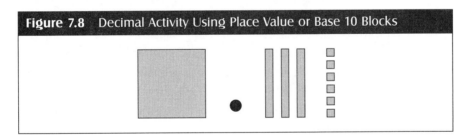

Figure 7.8 Decimal Activity Using Place Value or Base 10 Blocks

TEACHING THE "HOW TO COMPUTE" WITH FRACTIONS AND DECIMALS

Fractions

Because some students have a great deal of difficulty with fractions, it is important to think about how to teach them effectively. The techniques below follow the RTI Math Practice Guide Panel (Gersten et al., 2009) recommendation for visual representation when intervening. The fractions strategies displayed help teachers instruct how to represent and calculate fractions, including those with negative answers. It is important to know that these strategies are a sample of what is possible and the model shown here can be used for a great multitude of additional fractions problems.

1. Teach division of fractions using materials that can be cut or torn into fractions of the original unit. In Figure 7.9, five paper squares are divided into two containers. Since each container must hold equal amounts for accurate division, two went into each container with one remaining. To create the fraction version of one piece of paper divided into two containers, the piece is torn in half. The end result is 2½ pieces of paper per container. Thus 5 papers / 2 containers equal 2½ pieces of paper per container.

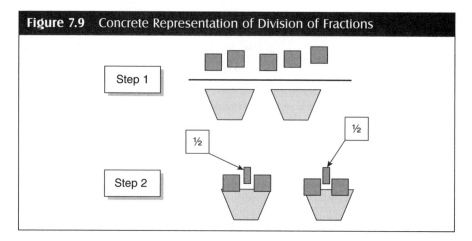

Figure 7.9 Concrete Representation of Division of Fractions

2. Use easy-to-manipulate concrete objects to teach equivalent and simplification of fractions (Witzel & Riccomini, 2009). In Figure 7.10, two sticks are placed over five sticks. To obtain an equivalent fraction, place down another numerator (2 sticks) and another denominator (5 sticks). Now there are 4 sticks / 10 sticks as there are two sets (×2) of the numerator and two sets (×2) of the denominator. Students can continue to build equivalent fractions by placing down another set of the numerator and another set of the denominator. Now there are 6 sticks over 15 sticks because there are three sets (×3) of the numerator and three sets (×3) of the denominator. Make the process obvious and introduce the identity principle of multiplying 1 set over 1 set.

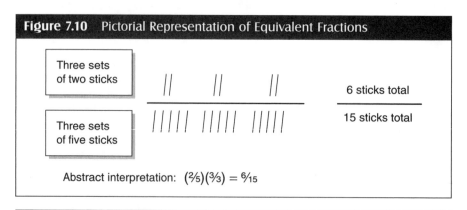

Figure 7.10 Pictorial Representation of Equivalent Fractions

Source: Adapted from Witzel, B., & Riccomini, P. J. (2009). *Computation of fractions: Math interventions for elementary and middle grades students.* Upper Saddle River, NJ: Pearson Education, Inc.

To simplify the fraction, group numerator and denominator sticks by the same number of sticks.

3. In a method similar to building equivalent fractions, use objects like pretzel sticks to add and subtract fractions with like and unlike denominators. First, set up the fractions as stated in the number sentence. For the example below, the number of sticks matches the numbers in the numerator and denominator. Then, equivalent fractions are made to match the numerators between the two fractions. Once the denominators are equal, the addition or subtraction operation can occur. Raise the sign to the numerator and compute those and those alone. In this example, 3 sticks + 1 stick are 4 sticks. The answer is 4 sticks over 6 sticks and then simplified to $\frac{2}{3}$. See Figure 7.11 for $\frac{1}{2} + \frac{1}{6}$.

Figure 7.11 Pictorial Representation for Adding Fractions

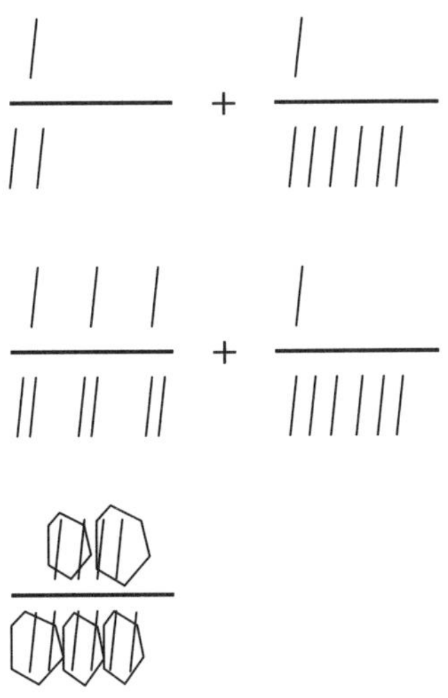

Abstract interpretation: $\frac{1}{2} + \frac{1}{6}$

$$\left(\tfrac{1}{2}\right)\left(\tfrac{3}{3}\right) + \tfrac{1}{6} =$$

$$\tfrac{3}{6} + \tfrac{1}{6} = \tfrac{4}{6}$$

$$\tfrac{4}{6} \div \tfrac{2}{2} = \tfrac{2}{3}$$

Source: Adapted from Witzel, B., & Riccomini, P. J. (2009). *Computation of fractions: Math interventions for elementary and middle grades students*. Upper Saddle River, NJ: Pearson Education, Inc.

4. Understanding that fractions can be negative is important for future use in algebraic computation. Using the same form of representation as above, the student sets up the problem as $\frac{1}{5} - \frac{4}{5}$. Knowing that the denominators are equal, the student turns to the numerator. He takes one out of each denominator and is left with $\frac{0}{5} - \frac{3}{5}$. This is interpreted

as $-\frac{3}{5}$. The purpose of such calculations is to learn that the same model for calculating positive fractions works with negative fractions (see Figure 7.12).

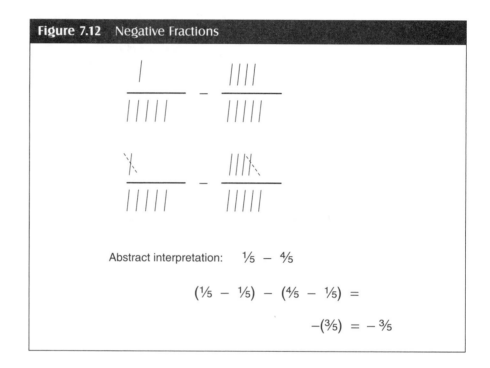

Figure 7.12 Negative Fractions

Abstract interpretation: $\frac{1}{5} - \frac{4}{5}$

$$(\frac{1}{5} - \frac{1}{5}) - (\frac{4}{5} - \frac{1}{5}) =$$

$$-(\frac{3}{5}) = -\frac{3}{5}$$

Source: Adapted from Riccomini, P. J., & Witzel, B. S. (2009). *Computation of integers: Mathematics interventions for middle and high school students.* Upper Saddle River, NJ: Pearson Education, Inc.

5. Multiplication of fractions can also be completed using hands-on and pictorial representations. The example below (Figure 7.13) shows how an array can be used to show multiplication of fractions. The use of an array follows the use of fraction strips since two fractions can be represented horizontally and vertically similarly to how fraction strips are represented. The example below shows $\frac{1}{3} \times \frac{1}{4}$. The answer is 1 square shaded out of 12 total squares or $\frac{1}{12}$.

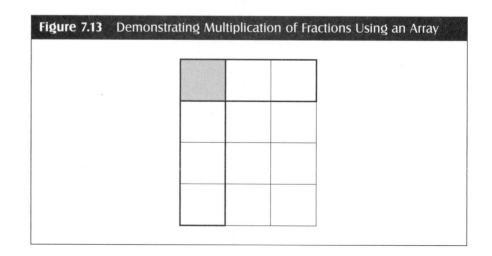

Figure 7.13 Demonstrating Multiplication of Fractions Using an Array

Decimals

Using concrete and pictorial models also works for decimals. The models below provide examples of how to intervene when teaching how to multiply and representing decimals. With these models, a teacher can expand to build more and different equations that can be applied to the Tier 1 classroom or the Tier 2 or 3 intervention classroom.

1. Using arrays also works for multiplication with decimals. Create grids that match base 10. See the example below (Figure 7.14) for 0.5×0.9. Shade the first decimal horizontally and the second decimal vertically. Then make a rectangle by connecting the end points of the two decimal representations. The total shaded area is the answer. The area of this example is 45 shaded out of 100, or 0.45.

Figure 7.14 Demonstrating Multiplication of Decimals Using an Array

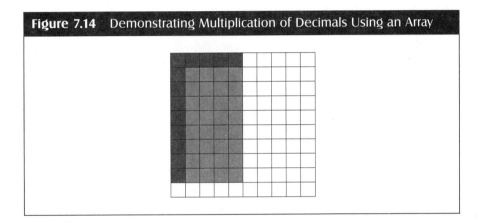

2. Expanded notation is another possible way to represent decimals in computation. In the two examples in Figure 7.15, the place value of the decimals are represented by a referent and the computation follows. This organization helps with borrowing, regrouping, and number alignment.

Figure 7.15 Representing Decimals Using Expanded Notation

2.53	2u	+	5tths	+	3hths
+ 0.68	+ 0u	+	6tths	+	8hths
	2u		11tths		11hths

2
+ 1.1
+ 0.11
3.21

1.5	$1.0 \times 0.9 =$	0.9
$\times 2.9$	$1.0 \times 2.0 =$	2.0
	$0.5 \times 0.9 =$	0.45
	$0.5 \times 2.0 =$	+ 1.0
		4.35

TEACHING FLUENCY WITH FRACTIONS AND DECIMALS

The NMAP pushes for proficiency with fractions. Thus, it is important to be accurate but it is also important to be fluent. The same principles that worked for teaching calculation fluency work for fractions and decimals. When working with physical objects, students must learn to work as quickly as physically possible using accurate and coordinating verbal description of the activity. For example, as a student is folding a fraction strip, he should describe the numerator and denominator as represented by the folds and shading.

Just like working with physical representations, when a student works with pictorial representations, he should be expected to use accurate, coordinating, and fluent verbalizations of his work on paper. When a student is drawing a decimal array, she should explain how the number of tenths is represented. These verbal representations are considered coordinating because they explain the why and how of the work that is being completed. Learning "why and how" helps the student gain fluency at the abstract level where he should become proficient. Thinking quickly about the problem solving is a precursor to acting quickly. For example, once a student learns to represent a decimal, such as one and twenty-five hundredths, with a physical object and pictorial representation in a place value manner, that same student will be able to solve a problem when asked abstractly, using Arabic numerals, 1.25.

IN CONTEXT

Fractions and decimals are used throughout our lives. Show students the usefulness of fractions and decimals and make them interact with fractions and decimals in school, at home with their parents, on the way to school, and through media. For interventions at the Tier 2 and 3 levels, it is important to concentrate instructional goals as appropriate per grade level and standard. As students progress in grade level, increase the focus on interventions on the computational aspects of fractions and decimals.

SUMMARY

This chapter explained the increased interest in learning decimals and fractions, which is due to the impact that fractions and decimals have on later understanding of mathematics. Much of this chapter showed instructional strategies for teaching fractions and decimals using visual and concrete representations as well as expanded forms that have been shown to be helpful to students with math difficulties. RTI models must develop an emphasis on preparing and intervening with usually complex math skills, such as fractions and decimals.

Teaching Problem Solving Strategically 8

When one interacts with the world or uses language to understand it, one engages in problem solving.

—Allsopp, Kyger, & Lovin, 2007, p. 136

Problem solving in mathematics requires a multiplicity of knowledge and skills blended together in harmony. Just like in music, if a note or chord is played incorrectly or in the wrong place, the music does not sound good. When students are unable to fluently blend the necessary knowledge and skills together when solving math problems, problem solving becomes very difficult. As students progress through their math education, problem solving becomes more and more important and complicated. When students have no or ineffective strategies to approach math problems, they become frustrated and give up quickly. Students require instruction in strategies that can promote better problem-solving skills. This chapter provides a brief description of three scientifically validated mathematical programs that teach problem solving strategically.

PROBLEM-SOLVING PROGRAMS

Hot Math, Pirate Math, and Solving Math Word Problems: Teaching Students With Learning Disabilities Using Schema-Based Instruction are three examples of evidence-based instructional practices used to improve math achievement by teaching students to solve problems strategically. In each of these programs, students are explicitly taught systematic strategies for solving math problems. General procedures for each program are described in the following section. This section is not intended to represent all problem-solving programs available, just a selected sample. See the following box for an example of a school's experience with Hot Math.

Teachers' Experience With Using Hot Math to Teach Problem Solving

 From the Teacher's Desk

By Kim Bingham and Karen Mellette
Third-Grade Teachers at Tom Joy Elementary in Nashville, Tennessee

We Love the Vanderbilt Problem-Solving Program at Tom Joy!

The Hot Math Program has really helped our students with their problem-solving math skills. During the lessons, students are excited, motivated, and actively engaged in the learning process. Before implementing Hot Math, problem solving was always something that our students had a hard time mastering, but now because of this well-designed program, our students really learn useful strategies that help them to became successful math problem solvers.

The part of the program that students enjoy the most is keeping track of their progress on their student thermometers. With each skill there are five thermometers. At the end of the each lesson, students are given the opportunity to do a problem individually. While working these problems, the students have to be careful and use the strategies presented to them during each skill in order to solve the problems correctly. They are given points for each part they get correct. Their points are then totaled. The fun part for the students is shading in their points on their thermometers. Students are challenged each week to make their thermometers rise higher and higher so they will become Hot in math.

We like how the program teaches different strategies and skills that help the students attack those ever-challenging word problems. One skill that we believe to be useful is called transfer. The students are taught that not all word problems are presented in the same way: some problems can look different, have different words or different questions, or might be a small piece of a bigger problem. Since most of the problems are represented in this way on the state achievement test, being able to transfer enables our students to become better problem solvers in the classroom as well as to perform better on the test.

The students really enjoy this fantastic program! Upon completing the program, they are more confident in their ability to solve a wider variety of math word problems. The Vanderbilt problem-solving program does indeed make students Hot in math.

Source: From Fuchs, L. S., & Fuchs, D. (Winter, 2002). Hot Math: Promoting mathematical problem solving among children with disabilities. *CASL News: Promoting Success in Grades K–3, 7,* 1–4. Reprinted with permission.

Hot Math

Hot Math is a 15-week program designed to promote mathematical problem-solving ability for third-grade students with disabilities. The program is available in a manual that includes teaching scripts and all necessary materials for implementing all units. The individual lessons within each unit are approximately 25–40 minutes in length. The program is organized into five 3-week units and is designed around two core principles: (1) explicit instruction about transfer and (2) self-regulated strategies (Fuchs & Fuchs, 2002).

For students to be successful in the Hot Math program, three main goals must be learned. First, students must learn the rules for solving the four main categories of problems taught in the program. Second, students must recognize and then classify problems into categories that require the similar solution steps. Third, students must put together new problems with familiar problems they already can solve (Fuchs & Fuchs, 2002). The program is design to teach students the three main goals through principles of systematic and explicit instruction.

Each lesson includes teacher modeling and opportunities for think aloud both by the teacher and with teacher support. Initially, the teacher is modeling the solution through a think-aloud process. Students have the opportunity to hear the teacher reason through the problem solution and verify that the solution is reasonable and makes sense. The problem solutions are gradually faded out thus allowing students multiple opportunities to provide parts of the solution with teacher feedback and support. As students become more confident, they have the opportunity for guided practice by working with a peer of higher ability who can provide corrective feedback and prompts as necessary. Finally, each lesson concludes with the students working one problem independently and then checking their solution against a key. Additionally, cumulative reviews are systematically incorporated throughout the units and homework is directly linked to the lesson objective. The explicit and systematic approach of the program makes it especially effective for students with disabilities as well as students who are struggling with problem-solving tasks.

The program is organized into units with the first unit focusing on basic problem-solving steps such as reasonableness of the answer, does the answer make sense, proper alignment of numbers for execution of the math operation, and labeling answers with appropriate symbols. After the first unit, each subsequent 3-week unit focuses on one of four problem types: (1) shopping list problems, (2) half problems, (3) buying bags problems, and (4) pictograph problems. Figure 8.1 provides examples of the four problem types addressed in Hot Math. The first four lessons focus on teaching students how to determine what the problem is asking and how to solve the problem. Once students are successful in the first four lessons of each unit, the last two lessons are devoted to teaching transfer.

Transfer is explicitly taught through three steps. First, students are taught the meaning of the word "transfer." Teachers provide students multiple examples in and out of math to demonstrate the meaning of transfer and why it is important. Second, once students understand the meaning of transfer, teachers explicitly teach four ways in which problem features can change a problem without changing the solution. Figure 8.2 (on p. 111) illustrates the four ways a problem can be changed and is also an example of a poster provided with the program. Students are then given opportunities to practice classifying problems according to which feature has changed and explain how problems look different but still correspond to the same problem type. Finally, students are encouraged to find opportunities outside

Figure 8.1 Example of Four Problem Types Taught in Hot Math

Example of Each of Four Problem Types for Which Solution Rules Are Taught

Shopping List Problem Type

Danny needs to buy things for his science projects. He needs 2 batteries, 3 wires, and 4 magnets. The batteries cost $3 each, the wires cost $3 each, and the magnets cost $2 each. How much money does Danny need for his science project?

Half Problem Type

Dave and Todd are going to buy a large box of baseball cards. There are 42 cards in the box. Dave and Todd will each get ½ of the cards. How many cards will each of them get?

Bag Problem Type

You want to buy some lemon drops. Lemon drops come in bags with 10 lemon drops in each bag. How many bags of lemon drops should you buy to get 32 lemon drops?

Pictograph Problem Type

Gloria collects teddy bears. She made a chart to show how many teddy bears she had. Each picture of a bear stands for 4 bears.

For her birthday, Gloria got 3 more teddy bears. How many bears does she have now?

Source: From Fuchs, L. S., & Fuchs, D. (Winter, 2002). Hot Math: Promoting mathematical problem solving among children with disabilities. *CASL News: Promoting Success in Grades K–3, 7,* 1–4. Reprinted with permission.

of math class where they might transfer what they learned in math to other situations (Fuchs & Fuchs, 2002). In addition to the explicit instruction about transfer, the program also facilitates the development of self-regulation within students. For information specifically about Hot Math and other Tier 1 and Tier 2 interventions, contact flora.murray@vanderbilt.edu.

Pirate Math

Pirate Math is a 16-week tutoring program designed to supplement the core mathematics curriculum and teaches mathematical problem solving to second- and third-grade students. The program is available in a manual that includes teaching scripts and all necessary materials for implementing the lessons. The individual lessons within each unit are approximately 25–30 minutes in length and

Figure 8.2   Example of Superficial Problem Features Taught in Hot Math

Superficial Problem Features Taught in the Transfer Treatment Illustrated With the Bag Problem Type

Original Problem

You want to buy some lemon drops. Lemon drops come in bags with 10 lemon drops in each bag. How many bags should you buy to get 32 lemon drops?

Different Format

➤ You want to buy some lemon drops.
➤ The sign at the store looked like this:

> **LEMON DROPS ON SALE!!!**
>
> 10 in each bag!!

How many bags should you buy to get 32 lemon drops?

   3   4   2   5

Different Key Word

You want to buy some lemon drops. Lemon drops come in packages with 10 lemon drops in each package. How many packages should you buy to get 32 lemon drops?

Additional Question

You want to buy some lemon drops. Lemon drops come in bags with 10 lemon drops in each bag. How many bags should you buy to get 32 lemon drops? If each bag costs $4, how much money will you spend?

Larger Problem-Solving Context

You saved $37. Your friend saved $12. You and your friend want to buy some lemon drops. Lemon drops come in bags with 10 lemon drops in each bag. You want 32 lemon drops.

1. How much money do you and your friend have?

2. If each bag of lemon drops costs $4, how much money will you spend on lemon drops?

3. If you also buy a hat that costs $15, how much money will you have left?

Source: From Fuchs, L. S., & Fuchs, D. (Winter, 2002). Hot Math: Promoting mathematical problem solving among children with disabilities. *CASL News: Promoting Success in Grades K–3, 7,* 1–4. Reprinted with permission.

take place three times a week. The lessons are organized into five activities and use a pirate theme to capture student interest. Additionally, the activities blend peer tutoring and teacher-directed strategy instruction to promote problem-solving skills in students who have experienced problems in the past (Seethaler, Powell, & Fuchs, n.d.).

In the first activity, Math Fact Flash Cards, students are allotted 1 minute to read through a stack of addition and subtraction flash cards. Students are taught a "count-up" strategy to use when a mistake is made on a math fact. The count-up strategy for addition includes three steps: (1) Put the bigger number in your head and say it, (2) count up the smaller number on your fingers, and (3) the last number you say is the answer. A similar count-up strategy for subtraction also includes three steps: (1) Put the minus number in your head and say it, (2) count up your fingers to the number you started with, and (3) the answer is the number of fingers you have up. A specific self-correction strategy provides students an appropriate strategy when a mistake is made and diminishes guessing. At the end of 1 minute, another minute is given for the student to try to beat the number of flash cards answered correctly in the first round. This activity is completed with a tutor and takes 2–4 minutes.

During the second activity, Word Problem Warm-Up, students are asked to explain how to solve a word problem from the previous lesson. This provides students with an opportunity to engage in mathematical communication in a think-aloud activity. It also serves to reteach and/or review the content from the previous lesson. This activity takes 2–3 minutes. During the main activity, Lesson, students are instructed in a strategy for solving problems. Initially, this is where students are taught the count-up strategy in addition and subtraction. As the student progresses through the program, the lesson focuses on teaching students to recognize three problem types: (1) total—involves the combining of two parts to equal a total, (2) difference—involves a bigger number and a smaller number being subtracted to find a difference, and (3) change—involves starting with an amount and an action resulting in an increase or decrease to find an ending amount. Students are instructed on a three-step strategy to determine the problem type. The strategy is called RUN and prompts students to **R**ead the problem, **U**nderline the question, and **N**ame the problem type. Once the problem type is determined, students progress through three questions that guide the student to set up the correct number sentence and execute the appropriate operation. This activity takes approximately 15 minutes.

The fourth activity, Sorting Cards, provides students additional practice opportunities for classifying problems into one of the three problem types. Flash cards containing word problems are read by the tutor and the student then identifies the problem type and places the card on a sorting mat. Any problems that were incorrectly classified are reviewed at the end of the activity to make sure students recognize their mistake. This activity generally takes 3 minutes. In the final activity, Pirate Problems, students have the opportunity to solve algebraic equations and word problems. One side of the paper has algebraic computation problems and the other side contains a word problem. Teachers are closely monitoring students as they work in pairs and provide immediate corrective feedback when necessary. This activity lasts about 5 minutes.

In addition to the instruction in problem solving, students are also rewarded with "treasure coins" throughout the lessons for following directions, listening, completing assigned activities, and improving their accuracy. At the end of the lesson, students color in a treasure map based on the number of coins earned, and once the map is completely colored, the student earns a small prize from an actual treasure test.

The Pirate Math program was developed as part of a 5-year study funded by the National Institute of Child Health and Human Development. For information regarding Pirate Math, contact Pamela.m.seethaler@vanderbilt.edu or sara.r.powell@vanderbilt.edu.

Solving Math Word Problems: Teaching Students With Learning Disabilities Using Schema-Based Instruction

The Solving Math Word Problems program is a carefully designed teacher-directed program used to teach critical word problem–solving skills to students with disabilities in the elementary and middle grades (Jitendra, 2007). The program includes eight units (five units—addition and subtraction problems; and three units—multiplication and division problems), and each unit includes three to five lessons. Lessons last approximately 30–60 minutes. The program is based on a well-researched strategy, schema-based instruction, which facilitates both conceptual understanding and procedural knowledge, both essential to successful problem solving.

The program contains four main parts: (1) Students are taught to recognize types of word problems—change, group, and compare for addition and subtraction; multiplicative compare; and vary for multiplication and division; (2) students are taught to translate the important information into a corresponding diagram for each problem type; (3) students are taught a series of rules to correctly determine the mathematics operation needed to solve a specific problem type; and (4) students are taught to compute the problem. These four steps are represented in a mnemonic, FOPS, to help students remember the steps. The following box illustrates the FOPS mnemonic. The program systematically and explicitly progresses students through a highly scaffolded series of teacher-directed instructional lessons that provide students a very strong strategy to approach math word problems.

FOPS Mnemonic Used to Help Students Remember the Steps for Problem Solving

Step 1: *F*ind the problem type.

Step 2: *O*rganize the information in the problem using the diagram (change, group, or compare).

Step 3: *P*lan to solve the problem

Step 4: *S*olve the problem.

Source: From A. K. Jitendra. (2007). *Solving math word problems: Teaching students with learning disabilities using schema-based instruction.* CD of printable forms (p. 297). Austin, TX: PRO-ED. Copyright 2007 by PRO-ED, Inc. Reprinted with permission.

The strength of the Solving Math Word Problems program lies within the instructional design features used throughout each lesson. This program provides teachers an appropriate scaffolding of instruction that includes a blend of teacher-mediated instruction, paired-partner learning, and independent practice activities. Initially, the word problems start as story situations, not questions. An example of a story situation is as follows: *Tyler has 37 Star Wars cards on Tuesday. He gives his sister 5 cards on Wednesday. Tyler now has 32 Star Wars cards.* By presenting story situations instead of word problems, students are better able to focus their attention to conceptually understand the mathematics representing the word situation. As students become fluent with the recognition and classification of story situations, the lessons gradually move into actual word problems; for example, *Tyler has some Star Wars cards; he gives his sister 5 cards. Now Tyler has 32 Star Wars cards. How many cards did he have before he gave his sister the cards?* The program systematically progresses students from story situations to word problems.

The program has diagrams and checklists that help students map the important information from the story situation or word problem into a diagram that eventually helps students solve the problem. Initially, teachers model the use of the diagrams and provide sufficient opportunities for students to practice mapping story situations and eventually word problems into the corresponding diagrams. Each problem type has a corresponding diagram to help highlight the most critical aspects of the word problems. As students progress through the lessons, the use of the checklists and diagrams are gradually faded out. This gradual fading out from story situations to word problems and away from diagrams and checklists promotes students' independent problem-solving ability at both the conceptual and procedural levels.

SUMMARY

Several common instructional design features are apparent across all three programs and include (a) explicit teacher-directed instruction, (b) opportunities to hear and participate in think-aloud activities, (c) gradual fading out of stories as solutions to problems, (d) high levels of scaffolding either by the teacher or from a peer, (e) multiple opportunities for both guided and independent practice with corrective feedback, (f) systematic cumulative reviews, (g) a reward system and/or positive reinforcement, (h) structured peer-tutoring activities, (i) a form of progress monitoring, and (j) clear and specific problem-solving methods. All the instructional features included in these three programs are common themes throughout the research on effective instructional strategies and methods for teaching math to struggling students and students with learning disabilities (e.g., Gersten et al., 2009; Jayanthi et al., 2008; Kroesbergen & Van Luit, 2003; NMAP, 2008; Newman-Gonchar et al., 2009). As a result of the strong research support, we encourage the use of each of the three problem-solving instructional programs described in this chapter.

The Importance of Teaching Mathematical Vocabulary 9

If students do not understand the language of instruction, they can't learn what is being taught.

—Paul J. Riccomini, 2009 (personal quote)

On more than one occasion during math instruction as a high school self-contained special education teacher, we can remember asking students to define *numerator* and *denominator.* Some of the most common and, unfortunately, eye-opening answers from students were (a) "top number," (b) "bottom number," (c) "always 1," and (d) "the top number is always smaller than the bottom number." Although the numerator is the top number and the denominator is the bottom number and sometimes the top number is 1, none of these common responses were correct. Moreover, some students would just give examples such as ½, ¼, and point to what they thought were the numerator and denominator. It became very clear that students' limited understanding of essential vocabulary was possibly impacting conceptual and procedural knowledge, problem-solving ability, and likely overall mathematical proficiency.

When students are unable to understand the language of instruction, they cannot learn what is being taught. Mathematical vocabulary can have a significant positive and/or negative impact on mathematical proficiency. This chapter provides an overview of the importance of teaching vocabulary and general and specific guidelines for teaching mathematical vocabulary. It is worth noting that the recommendations contained within this chapter are not necessarily specific to any one instructional tier, but rather should be incorporated across all tiers of instruction.

THE IMPORTANCE OF TEACHING MATHEMATICAL VOCABULARY

Problem-solving proficiency in mathematics depends on a combination of many essential mathematical skills and concepts, but it also requires students to use and understand mathematical language. The ability of students to effectively use and understand language in any content area is dependent on one's vocabulary knowledge (Baker, Simmons, & Kame'enui, 1997). The importance of mathematical language is evident in the National Research Council's (2001) five strands of mathematical proficiency, which include (1) understanding mathematics, (2) computing fluently, (3) applying concepts to solve problems, (4) reasoning logically, and (5) engaging in mathematics. Engaging in mathematics is more than just the application of concepts and procedures; it is the all-around ability to communicate mathematically.

Mathematics is a language (Adams, 2003; Raiker, 2002) that often uses very technical and context-specific terms (e.g., isosceles, scalene, minuend, subtrahend) and symbols (e.g., $\div$, $\geqslant$, $\neq$, $\prod$), which requires that learners develop the necessary vocabulary to communicate and understand mathematical language (Riccomini, Sanders, & Jones, 2008). It is estimated that by fourth grade as many as 500 technical mathematical terms and symbols have been used (Wilmon, 1971). Clearly, the importance of learning mathematical vocabulary is vital for students' ability to apply various mathematical concepts and skills to solve problems proficiently. Teachers should devote instructional time to essential mathematical vocabulary. The following sections provide both general and specific recommendations for teaching mathematical vocabulary.

General Guidelines for Teaching Mathematical Vocabulary

The importance of vocabulary in the area of mathematics is underestimated. Unfortunately, vocabulary instruction in math class is often overlooked or taught simultaneously with concepts or procedures. For many students, vocabulary must be directly taught and explicitly connected to meaningful contexts. Foil and Alber (2002) describe four general guidelines for teaching vocabulary that strengthen comprehension and capture student interest:

1. Employ a variety of methods and strategies.

2. Actively involve students in vocabulary instruction.

3. Provide instruction that enables students to see how target vocabulary words relate to other words.

4. Provide frequent opportunities to practice reading words in many contexts to help students gain a deeper and automatic comprehension of those target words.

Although each guideline is simple and self-explanatory, guideline four—providing frequent opportunities to practice—warrants further discussion.

Providing students with frequent opportunities to practice using important vocabulary is especially important in mathematics. The more opportunities students have to hear, read, speak, and use math vocabulary, the more likely it is that they learn the vocabulary and its appropriate context. Teachers must remember that the only time students will engage (e.g., hear, read, speak, use) in the language of math is during math class. Students are not likely to discuss isosceles and scalene triangles outside of math class, which reduces the opportunities to speak and hear math language. Use any opportunity to encourage students to use essential math vocabulary outside of class.

For example, many first-grade teachers as a standard practice send home a list of words for students to practice at home. The words sent home are generally high-frequency words important for developing early reading skills. Often, the words are written on 3 × 5 index cards and include a variety of important words (e.g., *said, I, there*) for first-grade students to learn. Students are responsible (with parental help of course) for practicing reading and spelling the words. Sometimes teachers even have a test or quiz at the end of the week. As former mathematics teachers, we wonder why teachers do not send home mathematics-related words; two or three a week could have a significant impact on students' vocabulary. Our own experience as parents of young children indicates that mathematical words are rarely (if ever) included in the list sent home; hence, a golden opportunity is missed to provide students an opportunity to use math-related terms. It is essential that teachers provide students multiple opportunities to learn and become fluent with important vocabulary early in their mathematics education. Although the focus of this book is on RTI and often Tier 2, strengthening the Tier 1 vocabulary instruction can greatly strengthen the other tiers.

Again, seek out any and all opportunities to increase engagement with important math vocabulary; there are many opportunities available that do not require a significant amount of effort and can have positive benefits. These general guidelines offer a starting point for teaching essential mathematics vocabulary; however, instruction must go much further than these four guidelines.

Specific Guidelines for Teaching Mathematical Vocabulary

Adding to the challenge of teaching mathematical vocabulary, many essential terms do not occur in context outside of math, and if they do, the meanings are often different. For example, a cone in math class has a very specific meaning, a solid shape with a circular base, but outside of math, a cone is a sweet cookie-like object that holds ice cream (Riccomini et al., 2008). Clearly, there are many variables that can impede learning math-related vocabulary.

Specific to teaching vocabulary in math class, Adams (2003) offers seven specific recommendations:

1. Establish a list of essential vocabulary words for each chapter or grade level.

2. Evaluate student comprehension of mathematical vocabulary on a periodic basis.

3. Probe students' previous knowledge and usage of important terms before they are introduced during instruction.

4. Frame the context for new mathematical vocabulary.

5. Develop an environment where mathematical vocabulary is a normal part of mathematics class.

6. Encourage students to ask about terms they don't know.

7. Teach students how to find meanings of vocabulary words.

Teachers incorporating these seven recommendations in their instruction are communicating to students that vocabulary is important and must be learned. When teachers fail to incorporate vocabulary into their daily instruction and assessment, they are indirectly communicating to students that vocabulary isn't that important in math class.

Creating a list of essential vocabulary by unit or by grade level is one of the best strategies for teachers to begin teaching students math terms. Many states are beginning to include vocabulary lists by grade levels within their math standards. Additionally, textbooks often come with lists of vocabulary words for each unit or chapter. Make sure the vocabulary list included in the textbook matches the list within the state standards. If the lists are different, special attention must be taken to make sure you are teaching and students are learning the vocabulary included on the state standards. It is these vocabulary words that are most likely to appear on end-of-year state assessments. A form for creating a list by unit of essential math vocabulary is contained in Table 9.1. Once a list of essential vocabulary is created, teachers can begin to explore various instructional strategies and activities to best teach students the vocabulary.

When students struggle or do not learn important mathematical vocabulary, they will likely not make important contextual connections, which leads to conceptual misconceptions. We presented five general guidelines for teaching vocabulary and then seven math-specific recommendations for teaching vocabulary. The guidelines and recommendations described above are a starting place for planning vocabulary instruction. They should become a standard part of math instruction and can be further strengthened by incorporating them into Tier 2 instructional supports. The next section describes six instructional strategies designed to promote learning and understanding of essential math vocabulary.

INSTRUCTIONAL ACTIVITIES TO PROMOTE LEARNING OF ESSENTIAL MATHEMATICAL VOCABULARY

Many students struggle to learn even the basic definitions of common mathematical vocabulary words. This lack of understanding can lead to conceptual

Table 9.1 Create a List of Essential Vocabulary for Mathematics Class

Unit Objective:

_____

_____

_____

_____

Key Vocabulary Terms	Definition (Include previous grade level if different.)	Examples and Nonexamples	Similar or Related Terms
Parallelogram	**insert definition consistent with your curriculum and/or state standards		Square, rectangle, quadrilateral, parallelogram, polygon

Note: Check previous grade-level and current grade-level state standards, teacher's guides, and test preparation or practice guides.

Source: Riccomini, P. J. (2009). *The importance of teaching vocabulary during math class.* Professional Development Workshop for Educators. Reprinted with permission.

and procedural errors and interfere with students' problem-solving ability. It is important for teachers to incorporate instructional activities routinely during mathematics instruction to increase comprehension of important vocabulary. Six specific instructional activities to facilitate deeper vocabulary understanding in your students are described here:

1. Use technology applications and resources.
2. Use directed journaling activities.
3. Teach word parts and origins.
4. Preteach vocabulary prior to the instructional lesson.
5. Provide practice opportunities to build fluency.
6. Use graphic organizers.

Technology Applications and Resources

The advances in technology applications for instructional purposes continue to evolve at a phenomenal rate as does increased access to technology. Most classroom teachers have Internet access and at least one computer in the classroom with many teachers having access to SMART Boards and Promethean Boards. These technologies combined with the Internet can be a powerful and motivating instructional tool for teaching math vocabulary. Teaching students how to use technology to explore math vocabulary can be very useful to both students and teachers.

Obviously, students can use the glossary provided at the end of a textbook to look up definitions, but a vast resource of online tools is also available. *A Maths Dictionary for Kids* (www.amathsdictionaryforkids.com) provides students an interactive, easy-to-use online dictionary devoted solely to mathematics (see Figure 9.1). The dictionary provides animated and interactive definitions, examples, activities, and practice in a kid-friendly format that most children will find interesting. For example, the term "array" is defined as a set of objects or numbers in order, often in rows and columns. When students click on the word "array," the definition is displayed, and below the definition is an interactive activity that allows students to click on certain objects that are then displayed in an array. In another example, when students click on the word "number line," a definition is provided and an interactive activity allows students to enter in two numbers to form an addition problem. The numbers and the answer are displayed on a number line. This type of resource is not only informative for students but is also motivating and may lead students to access it on their own.

Figure 9.1   A Maths Dictionary for Kids

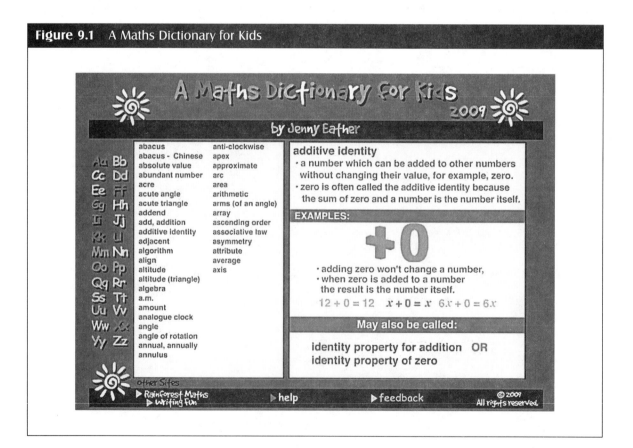

Directed Journaling Activities

When students solve a math problem, they are demonstrating comprehension, very similar to students comprehending a story passage. In reading, comprehension is the ultimate goal; we want students to be able to ascertain information from written text. Problem solving in mathematics is also a type of comprehension. By correctly solving a problem, a student has demonstrated comprehension of certain mathematical concepts and procedures, vocabulary, and likely computational accuracy and fluency. Incorporating writing activities into math class is a way to improve mathematical comprehension and provides students opportunities to use language and vocabulary through writing.

It is important to note that teachers must use caution when asking students to write. For students who struggle and students with learning disabilities, writing is a very difficult task for many reasons. Students with learning disabilities generally have very poor spelling, smaller vocabularies—both receptive and expressive—and tend to use shorter sentences when asked to write. Initially, writing about math topics will be very difficult and will require a great deal of support or scaffolding by the teacher. It is better to begin this type of writing activity by giving students very specific questions to write about. Here are three examples:

1. What are the differences and similarities between parallelograms, rectangles, and squares?

2. Why is the area of a triangle ½ *bh,* and why is the area of a square s^2?

3. What happens to the circumference and area of a circle if the radius is doubled?

By providing students specific questions, teachers are better able to focus attention on important concepts, vocabulary, and connections. It is best to avoid open-ended questions such as (a) What did we learn today? (b) What was important about today's math lesson? or (c) How can fractions be applied to your daily lives? These questions are likely to generate answers such as "I don't know," "Who cares," or "Nothing, and this is stupid." Activities generating these types of questions are unproductive and a waste of time.

Support students' directed journal writing much the same way a reading teacher would support student writing during reading class. Provide students with word banks, outlines, charts, tables, concepts maps, and so on. The purpose of directed journaling is to provide students additional opportunities to engage in the language of mathematics. For example, a class of 25 students is given the following question:

- What happens to the circumference and area of a circle if the diameter is doubled?

Teachers know the strengths and weaknesses of their class; in this scenario, the teacher recognizes that three-fourths of the class will need some level of teacher support in order to complete this directed journaling activity.

To support those students, a chart is created and provided to students to support their writing in this activity. See Table 9.2 for the charts. The students who are very confident in their mathematics ability begin working immediately on the question and do not require the use of the chart; they will likely create a chart on their own as would most strategic learners.

The next group of students is not as confident, but they demonstrate solid math skills and strategic problem-solving skills, so a blank chart is provided (Chart A) as a prompt to help them answer the question in an organized fashion.

Table 9.2 (Chart A) Scaffolding a Directed Journaling Activity		
Radius	*Circumference* $C = 2\prod r$	*Area* $A = \prod r^2$
$r =$		
$r =$		
$r =$		
What is the relationship?		

Note: Chart can be modified to fit the specific situation and student instructional needs.

Source: Riccomini, P. J. (2009). *The importance of teaching vocabulary during math class.* Professional Development Workshop for Educators. Reprinted with permission.

The next group of students will require more support than the first two groups of students. This group of students enjoys mathematics, but the students demonstrate weaknesses in computation and lack confidence in their problem-solving ability; a partially completed chart (Chart B) and calculators are provided to help them answer the question. Since the purpose of this activity is not necessarily to calculate the circumference and area, but rather to recognize the relationship between the radius and circumference and area of a circle, calculators are an appropriate instructional tool in this activity.

Table 9.2 (Chart B) Scaffolding a Directed Journaling Activity		
Radius	*Circumference* $C = 2\prod r$	*Area* $A = \prod r^2$
$r = 2$ in	in	in^2
$r = 4$ in	in	in^2
$r = 8$ in	in	in^2
What is the relationship?		

Note: Chart can be modified to fit the specific situation and student instructional needs.

Source: Riccomini, P. J. (2009). *The importance of teaching vocabulary during math class.* Professional Development Workshop for Educators. Reprinted with permission.

The next group of students is not the weakest in the class, but they lack fundamental computation skills, problem-solving skills, and are easily discouraged (i.e., give up quickly); a completed chart (Chart C) is provided to help them solve the problem. Four circles cut out of construction paper with radii of 2 inches, 4 inches, and 8 inches are also provided to these students to provide a concrete example of the circles to assist in recognition of the relationship.

Table 9.2 (Chart C) Scaffolding a Directed Journaling Activity		
Radius	Circumference $C = 2\prod r$	Area $A = \prod r^2$
$r = 2$ in	$4\prod$ in	$4\prod$ in^2
$r = 4$ in	$8\prod$ in	$16\prod$ in^2
$r = 8$ in	$16\prod$ in	$64\prod$ in^2
What is the relationship?		

Note: Chart can be modified to fit the specific situation and student instructional needs.

Source: Riccomini, P. J. (2009). *The importance of teaching vocabulary during math class.* Professional Development Workshop for Educators. Reprinted with permission.

The weakest group is also the students who are most likely to disrupt the class when asked to complete independent activities. This group is provided a completed chart (Chart D) and the answer to the question. The teacher will take the students through the chart, highlighting the most critical attributes in the chart, and lead a discussion of the answer. Additionally, the teacher uses the construction paper circles described above and a string to concretely demonstrate the relationship of the circumference to the radii. After this teacher guidance, students can partner up and go over the chart and answer with their partner. Students are then given a blank sheet and asked to complete it as homework, and all groups are assigned to go home and explain the relationship to a household member.

There are several extensions to this activity. Students could complete a hands-on activity where they have to create circles with increasing radii to demonstrate the relationship concretely, or they could draw pictures of circles with increasing radii. If a SMART Board or Promethean Board is available, teachers could have students create their circles on the board in a motivating activity involving technology. Additionally, this writing activity could be completed through a classwide cooperative activity where partners are formed and work together to learn the relationship. In a coteaching setting, there are many possibilities for formatting this type of activity. This is just an example with hypothetical students and hypothetical supports (charts) that may or may not apply to your students; however, the principles of this activity can be applied to almost any learning situation.

Table 9.2 (Chart D) Scaffolding a Directed Journaling Activity		
Radius	Circumference $C = 2\prod r$	Area $A = \prod r^2$
$r = 2$ in	$4\prod$ in	$4\prod$ in^2
$r = 4$ in	$8\prod$ in	$16\prod$ in^2
$r = 8$ in	$16\prod$ in	$64\prod$ in^2
What is the relationship? As the radius is doubled, the circumference is also doubled. As the radius is doubled, the area is quadrupled.		

Note: Chart can be modified to fit the specific situation and student instructional needs.

Source: Riccomini, P. J. (2009). *The importance of teaching vocabulary during math class.* Professional Development Workshop for Educators. Reprinted with permission.

Teaching Word Parts and Origins

For older students, teaching word origins or meanings of word parts can help increase vocabulary comprehension. Take a moment the next time a spelling bee is on TV and notice that almost every contestant asks for the word to be used in a sentence, the meaning of the word, and the origin of the word; these are all clues that help eventually spell the word. Help students make connections by highlighting the words behind the words (Rubenstein, 2000; Schwartzman, 1994). Sometimes when students realize that parts of words have meanings, the entire word begins to make better sense and provides students context in which they can better remember definitions.

Preteaching Vocabulary Prior to Instructional Lesson

Probably one of the easiest and most effective strategies for helping students with vocabulary is to explicitly preteach difficult vocabulary prior to the instructional lesson. This helps students for at least two reasons. First, by preteaching the vocabulary word and corresponding definition, students are already familiar with the word when it is eventually encountered in the lesson. This frees up the students' cognitive processing capacity, so that they can better focus on the concept or procedure being taught. Second, when students are pretaught vocabulary words, it will help activate important prior knowledge that can help assimilate the new information presented in the lesson. There are five basic guidelines for explicitly preteaching vocabulary (IRIS Center, n.d.):

1. Pronounce the word for the students.

2. Clearly state the definition and have students repeat.

3. Provide multiple examples as well as nonexamples.

4. Review the new words as well as previously learned words to ensure that students do not forget the previously learned words.

5. Teach words within context.

Given the increasing numbers of cotaught classrooms, preteaching vocabulary should be a common instructional tool in the core mathematics program. Additionally, students who are receiving Tier 2 instructional supports could certainly have part of that time devoted to preteaching important and difficult-to-learn vocabulary. Preteaching vocabulary allows students to have a basic understanding prior to instruction and reduces barriers, but students also need multiple opportunities to use the word in order to gain fluency.

Practice Activities to Build Fluency With Important Mathematical Vocabulary

Students who struggle and students with learning disabilities sometimes have limited memory capacity. Practice is an important variable in the learning and remembering of mathematical vocabulary. The National Mathematics Advisory Panel (2008) recommends practice as a way to help students overcome limitations in memory and automatic recall. Practice activities should occur after instruction and once students are accurate with the definition and concept. The purpose of providing practice opportunities is to build fluency and maintain the vocabulary and definition in the students' repertoire. Opportunities for practice can occur in a variety of activities such as peer tutoring, small groups, independently, or in the *Jeopardy* game show style.

Let's revisit the example of the first-grade teacher sending home important words on 3 × 5 index cards (see Figure 9.2). This time, the first-grade teacher decided to include three math terms each week on the list that goes home. The teacher has the students write the terms on 3 × 5 cards with the definition on the back to take home and practice reading and saying the definitions. At the end of the week, the students are put into teams and play a *Jeopardy*-like game that focuses on the vocabulary. Additionally, 5 minutes at the beginning of each class are spent on an activity using the 3 × 5 index cards; sometimes the activity is spent in small groups, peer tutoring, or one-on-one for students struggling. Periodically, throughout the year, students have to locate the 3 × 5 index cards with vocabulary selected by their teacher and practice using it in a sentence and provide examples and nonexamples. In this scenario, the first-grade teacher strategically selected words for extra instruction and practice that are not only important but are often difficult to learn for some students. By systematically incorporating this kind of instructional focus on vocabulary, it is very likely that students will increase their vocabulary knowledge and comprehension and hopefully their problem-solving ability.

Index cards are not just for older children. Figure 9.3 contains an example of using index cards to teach students vocabulary terms for shapes. After

Figure 9.2 Example of Vocabulary Words on 3 × 5 Index Cards for Practice Activities

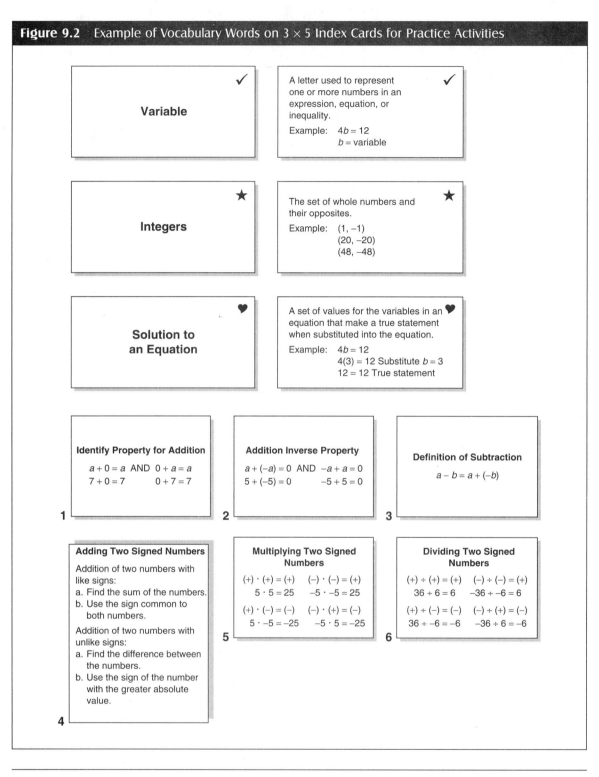

Source: Courtesy of the IRIS Center, Peabody College.

students receive initial instruction in the vocabulary word and its corresponding definition, students can easily and quickly continue to practice with the index card building and improving their fluency and automatic recall of the selected vocabulary.

Figure 9.3 Using Index Cards to Teach Vocabulary Terms Associated With Shapes

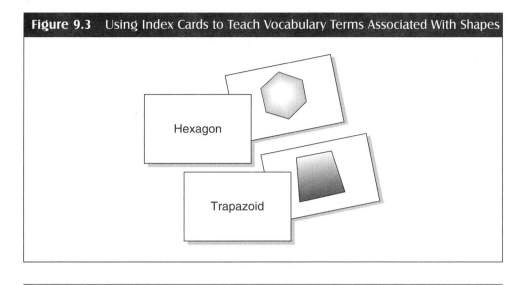

Source: Courtesy of the IRIS Center, Peabody College.

Graphic Organizers

Students who struggle and/or have learning disabilities are not very organized in their learning. Notes are often very messy, unorganized, and difficult to read. This is a barrier to learning because students have nothing to refer back to (i.e., notes) when trying to do independent work. Graphic organizers, sometimes called concepts maps, are a way to help students better organize their thoughts and information, which helps them recognize relationships between concepts (Ives & Hoy, 2003; Jitendra, 2002). Additionally, graphic organizers are very appealing and often a motivating alternative to standard note taking for students. Graphic organizers and concept maps can take many different shapes and forms, but all have one purpose in common: to help students better organize information so that relationships are more easily noticed. Figure 9.4 contains an example concept map for the term *exponent* (IRIS Center, n.d.). Notice that in the example provided on exponents, the graphic organizer includes the vocabulary needed in the definition of *exponent* as well as the mathematics behind an exponent.

The Frayer Model is another graphic organizer useful for teaching mathematical vocabulary. The Frayer Model organizes information into five parts: (1) target term, (2) definition, (3) characteristics, (4) examples, and (5) nonexamples (see Figure 9.5). This graphic organizer presents components of a new vocabulary word together in an easy-to-follow concept map. This allows students to see both examples and nonexamples of math terms as well as the technical definition and characteristics. The Frayer Model is designed to easily show both examples and nonexamples. The other positive aspect about the Frayer Model is that it can be used to teach vocabulary in other content areas (e.g., science, social studies), therefore allowing students to use a common structure to learn vocabulary across content classes.

Figure 9.4 Example Graphic Organizer for Exponents

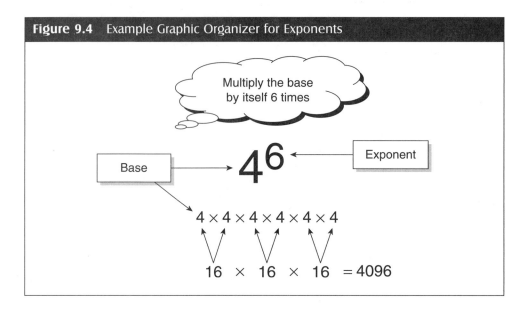

Source: Courtesy of the IRIS Center, Peabody College.

Figure 9.5 Example Frayer Model for Composite Numbers

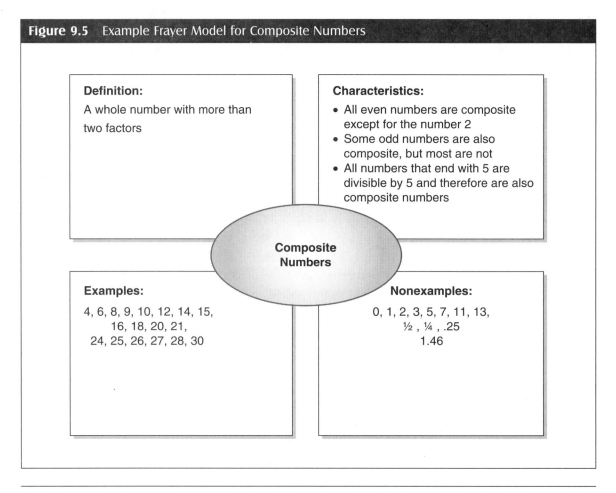

Source: Riccomini, P. J. (2009). *The importance of teaching vocabulary during math class.* Professional Development Workshop for Educators. Reprinted with permission.

We encourage the use of graphic organizers to help students learn important vocabulary and recognize relationships to other similar words (e.g., quadrilateral, parallelogram, square, and rectangle). There is no right or wrong graphic organizer, and once created, it becomes a permanent instructional tool that can be brought out any time for students to revisit and review.

ASSESSING STUDENTS' KNOWLEDGE OF MATHEMATICAL VOCABULARY

As we discussed in Chapter 2, assessment is an essential component of RTI procedures because it allows teachers to monitor students' progress or lack of progress and make timely and appropriate instructional decisions. Teachers can assess mathematical vocabulary in a variety of ways such as by including vocabulary questions on tests and quizzes. Teachers can also assess vocabulary through the use of a progress-monitoring format (Jones, 2001) designed specifically for vocabulary.

The purpose of progress monitoring is to measure student learning across a period of time on end-of-year goals. To measure growth in students' vocabulary knowledge, teachers can create short (2–3 minutes), timed assessments comprising words randomly selected from a master list of essential vocabulary students should have learned by the end of the year. The teacher would administer the assessments at least twice monthly to monitor student progress on learning of the essential vocabulary. When it is apparent certain words are continually missed on the progress-monitoring probes, teachers can focus additional instruction on those words. There are several steps to creating progress-monitoring probes for mathematical vocabulary.

First, create a master list of essential math vocabulary students are expected to have learned by the end of the school year. This list can be obtained from various sources including state standards, teachers' guides, and any other relevant sources. See Table 9.3 for a list of vocabulary words relating to number sense and operations students in third grade are expected to learn in New York.

Once a master list is created, develop 10–15 probes by randomly selecting 3–5 words for each probe. It is okay for a probe to contain vocabulary that the student hasn't received instruction on yet. Since the purpose is to measure progress, as more vocabulary words are taught, the students will know more words and score higher on the progress-monitoring probes. The probes can be elaborate in the questions asked or very simple. Table 9.4 contains an example of a simple progress-monitoring probe. This probe is very simple in that it is asking students to only write the definition and provide an example. For younger students, this probe could be administered orally. Scoring is also very simple: (a) correct definition equals one point and (b) providing a correct example equals one point. As students learn more and more vocabulary, students' scores are expected to increase. Students' progress can be displayed on a graph that the students manage, thus helping students take ownership in their learning.

Table 9.3 Example List of Third-Grade Math Vocabulary Words for Number Sense and Operations

Number Sense and Operations, Third Grade

array		number line
associative property		number sentence
commutative property of addition		numerator
commutative property of multiplication		numeric expression
compare		ones place
decimal		operational method/operation
denominator		order
difference		place value
digits		product
divide		property
dividend		quotient
division		reasonableness
divisor		regroup (regrouping)
doubling		related facts
equivalent		round (rounding)
equivalent fractions		set of objects
estimate		skip count
even number		subtract
expanded form		subtraction
factor		sum
fraction		tens place
halving		three-digit number
hundreds chart		unit fraction
hundreds place		value
identity element for multiplication		whole number
mental math		zero property of multiplication
multiple		
multiplication		
multiply		
number		

Source: New York State Education Department, *Suggested list of mathematical language for Grade 3.* Retrieved from http://www.emsc.nysed.gov/3-8/glossary.htm.

Table 9.4 Example of a Math Vocabulary Progress-Monitoring Probe

Name: _____

Probe #1: _____ Date: _____

Vocabulary Word	Definition	Provide an Example
Multiple		
Tens Place		
Equivalent		
Product		
Denominator		
		Score: _____

Teachers can gather a great deal of instructionally relevant information from progress monitoring students' vocabulary knowledge and then be better able to provide targeted instruction on difficult vocabulary. Including vocabulary during math instruction and assessments is essential for improving vocabulary instruction and the understanding of important mathematical vocabulary.

SUMMARY

Effective communication requires the use of language and comprehension of vocabulary. For students to understand, engage, and communicate using the language of mathematics, vocabulary understanding is critical. Many students fail to learn important and even fundamental mathematical vocabulary and struggle to reach proficiency. This chapter covered several methods to help students connect new and difficult vocabulary to appropriate mathematical context necessary for comprehension and, ultimately, proficiency. The recommendations made within this chapter are not specific to any instructional tier (1, 2, or 3), but they should be incorporated across all the instructional tiers.

Next Steps in the RTI Process 10

To survive and succeed, every organization will have to turn itself into a change agent. The most effective way to manage change successfully is to create it.

—Drucker, 2002

RTI holds great promise for helping students, even in mathematics. An effective RTI system may (a) lower misplaced LD student numbers, (b) reduce inappropriate referrals to special education and misidentified students in special education, (c) improve general education instruction, (d) set up a clear plan for helping all students reach their potential, and (e) organize a professional development model. However, an ineffective system may cause difficulty in each of these areas. Before initiating an RTI system, make certain that your district, school, teachers, and community are prepared.

Step1: Find or create an assessment system that allows for screening and progress monitoring. We highly discourage attempting to create an assessment because of the amount of effort that would be required to create a reliable and valid assessment. Screening helps identify who needs help or who is finally succeeding. Monitoring student progress of standards or curricular task analyses help us make changes in our classrooms on a more frequent basis according to the instructional needs of the students.

Step 2: Not only must we decide what we want to call Tier 1 instructional delivery and curriculum, we must also implement it with fidelity. By using research and evidenced approaches to learning, we can focus on essential ways that help students learn. We know that explicit instruction is important when teaching new or difficult content. By analyzing how our students are performing, we can decide on which math components must be taught in a certain manner. To make certain that everyone agrees on this manner, it is important to have educators buy into the idea. However, we must also conduct group meetings and classroom visits to help educators, particularly resistant ones, understand how math should be taught. When success is found in the students' data, then repeat the same process with incremental improvements.

In regard to curriculum, we must examine the research to determine what is working for a majority of students. Once we decide on what to teach, we must implement it. However, we must also monitor the progress of the curriculum and make adjustments when necessary. Whenever possible, it is important to pilot and compare newer ideas in order to establish the perceived effectiveness.

Step 3: Deciding on an intervention system is important. A standard protocol of general instruction and tiered intervention helps establish rules and procedures that allow transparency for outside constituents to observe what is happening when students struggle and why they are struggling. While a standard protocol is easier to implement and monitor, there must still be an element of problem solving. Some students present unique challenges that will not be addressed systematically through the proposed standard protocol. Decide on how the RTI team will address specific student weaknesses when they are not being addressed in the standard protocol model.

Step 4: Review the research on interventions that meet the needs of your school or district. Interventions that can quickly help a student succeed with less support are the most desired. Examining detailed screening data can help show what areas are weakest in the district. At a minimum, these areas must be covered with research and evidence-supported interventions. Although well-selected interventions are important, their delivery is equally important. Teachers must be recruited and others trained who can effectively implement interventions with high fidelity. Also, environments must be made available where students can receive the extra help. Schedules need to be flexible enough to allow a flow from intervention to general education classes. Removing students from classes where they succeed is dangerous. Students must want to succeed and feel successful.

Step 5: Decide what your Tier 3 is meant to be and find a curricular match. If Tier 3 is meant to be for alternative curriculum standards, then find an effective program that prepares students for postsecondary success. If Tier 3 is more individualized and a more intensive intervention with the goal of eventually returning students to the general education classroom, then establish what is essential to their math future and intensely focus on that goal. Although evidenced curricula are scarce, continue to research what is successful.

Step 6: Review the effectiveness of the RTI system per student data and adjust the policies and procedures accordingly. It is often useful to establish a team of superior teachers and school leaders to review the school- and district-level RTI system and make necessary adjustments. Their work with the RTI system will not only help improve student learning, but their buy-in will help enforce treatment integrity and fidelity. Of more widespread importance is the need for research on interventions. Creating school-based action research models will help establish what works in each setting. Carefully selecting assessments and comparing interventions across each setting will help increase the validity of the findings. The larger and more controlled the study, the more reliable the findings might be. Publishing the results in peer-reviewed journals will help create a larger amount of research from which other districts and educators can draw in their own efforts to improve student learning.

PROFESSIONAL DEVELOPMENT

Use experts to help develop the RTI system. From Tier 1 instruction to Tier 2 and Tier 3 interventions, many of the ideas of RTI are difficult for everyone to understand and implement. Moreover, many math teachers may have been erroneously taught in their undergraduate education that one size fits all or that what they witnessed as K–12 students is effective for all students. Bring in experts to show how and even why teaching or intervening is done in a specific way. Training should show how to implement evidence-supported interventions that have a history of effectiveness with struggling students. Moreover, follow-up training and teacher "check-ins" where teachers report data and reflect as a team on instructional and curricular practices allow teachers to grow in their goal to improve student learning.

In the book *Managing in the Next Society*, Drucker (2002) stated, "To survive and succeed, every organization will have to turn itself into a change agent. The most effective way to manage change successfully is to create it." He goes on to say that "the point of becoming a change agent is that it changes the mind-set of the entire organization. Instead of seeing change as a threat, its people will come to consider it an opportunity." Although Drucker focused his life on business, his words speak loud and clear to educators. We know that we must change and we see where change is heading. There will be bumps along the way, but if we continue to focus on improving student learning, then general education, special education, and administration can work together to smooth the road for years to come.

RECONSIDERING THE TIER 1 MATHEMATICS CURRICULUM

Mathematics education is receiving more and more attention in today's standards-based education system. State departments of education are continually revamping, reorganizing, and increasing mathematics standards and requirements with the hopes of improving overall mathematics performance. As RTI models begin to focus on mathematics, educators are struggling with how best to deliver state standards to students who are struggling through the general education curriculum, Tier 1.

Currently, standard practice is for Tier 1 instruction to be based on the state standards. Generally speaking, Tier 1 is dictated by state standards and delivered through a commercially available mathematics curriculum issued by large publishers. Schools devote a large amount of time analyzing the mathematics curriculum to verify that it is aligned with their state's standards; when alignment is not apparent, districts may select another mathematics program or opt to supplement one of the programs high on their list. Regardless, once a mathematics curriculum is selected, it becomes the main vehicle for delivering state standards.

In some states, the decision on which mathematics curriculum best links with standards is made at the state level through the Department of Curriculum and Instruction. A list of "state-approved" mathematics curricula is then made available to all school districts. Then, individual school districts select from the state-approved list the mathematics curriculum program they will use. State adoptions typically go in 3- or 4-year cycles. Most school districts select one program from the state-approved list to use as their core mathematics program. This selected program then becomes the main instructional tool (i.e., core mathematics program) for delivering the state mathematics standards. Within current RTI models, the selected curriculum becomes the foundation (Tier 1) of the instructional tiered system used in an RTI model. All other decisions are then based on and extended from that particular mathematics program. This would not be a problem if all commercially available curriculum programs were equal; they are certainly not! As we discussed in Chapter 2, the importance of the core mathematics program is enormous.

Research investigating the effectiveness of commercially available mathematics curriculum programs is beginning to emerge with results that cannot be ignored, especially by educators who correlate student scores to the curriculum, such as in typical RTI procedures. Recently, researchers are reporting that the instructional approach on which the program is based and designed can positively and/or negatively influence mathematical performance (see boxed text that follows). Interestingly enough, some approaches are not only impacting students with disabilities and/or who are struggling but are also influencing the achievement of average-performing students (Agodini, Harris, Atkins-Burnett, Heaviside, Novak, & Murphy, 2009). The point here is not to endorse or condemn any program, but rather to highlight the importance of selecting, correctly implementing, and evaluating a core mathematics program. It would be naïve to ignore the potential impact a core program has on student performance, especially students who continuously struggle, such as those with learning disabilities. We recognize the infancy and limitations of the Agodini study, but at the same time we recognize the potential impact of investigating core mathematics programs.

Instructional Approach of Math Curricula Can Impact Overall Student Math Performance

Results of an implementation study of the efficacy of four commercially available math curricula conducted by Mathematica Policy Research Inc. demonstrated that elementary schools using either Math Expressions or Saxon Math as the core program outperformed other schools that used Investigations in Number, Data, and Space or Scott Foresman-Addison Wesley Mathematics (SFAW) programs.

Main Findings

- Student math achievement was significantly higher in schools assigned to Math Expressions and Saxon than in schools assigned to Investigations and SFAW.
- The effect is strong enough that an average-performing student's percentile rank would improve by 9 to 12 points if the school used Math Expressions or Saxon, instead of Investigations or SFAW.

About the Curricula

Investigations in Number, Data, and Space, published by Pearson Scott Foresman, uses a student-centered approach to mathematics education. Its lessons focus on understanding, rather than on correct answers, and it builds on students' knowledge and understanding. Students engage in units of 3 to 8 weeks in which they first investigate then discuss and reason about problems and strategies.

Math Expressions, published by Houghton Mifflin Company, blends student-centered and teacher-directed approaches. Students question and discuss mathematics but are explicitly taught effective procedures. There is an emphasis on using multiple specified objects, drawings, and language to represent concepts, and an emphasis on learning through the use of real-world situations. Students are expected to explain and justify their solutions.

Saxon Math, published by Harcourt Achieve, is a scripted curriculum that blends teacher-directed instruction of new material with daily distributed practice of previously learned concepts and procedures. Students hear the correct answers and are explicitly taught procedures and strategies. Other key factors of the program include frequent monitoring of student achievement and extensive daily routines that emphasize practice of number concepts and procedures and use of representations.

Scott Foresman-Addison Wesley Mathematics, published by Pearson Scott Foresman, is a basal curriculum that combines teacher-directed instruction with a variety of differentiated materials and instructional strategies. Teachers select the materials that seem most appropriate for their students, often with the help of the publisher. The curriculum is based on a consistent daily lesson structure, which includes direct instruction, hands-on exploration, the use of questioning, and practice of new skills.

Source: Agodini, R., Harris, B., Atkins-Burnett, S., Heaviside, S., Novak, T., & Murphy, R. (2009). *Achievement effects of four early elementary school math curricula: Findings from first graders in 39 schools* (NCEE 2009-4052). Washington, DC: National Center for Education Evaluation and Regional Assistance, Institute of Education Sciences, U.S. Department of Education.

As we have discussed previously, there are two competing instructional approaches dominating the field of mathematics education: (1) teacher directed and (2) student centered. As a result, commercially available mathematics programs are designed based on one of these instructional approaches, with some programs attempting to combine both instructional approaches. Early curriculum comparisons, such as the study by Agodini and colleagues (2009), help us begin to show the impact of instructional approaches on student learning. We hope that more broad comparative evaluations of curriculum programs reach publication to aid in district Tier 1 decisions.

WHY IS THIS IMPORTANT FOR EDUCATORS IMPLEMENTING AN RTI MATH MODEL?

As we mentioned throughout the book, the most effective RTI model will have a very effective core mathematics program used in Tier 1. The selection of a well-designed core mathematics program is essential to the success of any RTI model in mathematics. Additionally, the National Mathematics Advisory Panel (2008) recommended that a balance between teacher-directed and student-centered instruction is needed. Research does not support the exclusive use of either approach, and the panel went on to recommend that students who struggle, are at risk for math difficulties, or have a disability that affects their math performance receive regular access to systematic and explicit methods of instruction (i.e., teacher-directed instruction). This recommendation is consistent with other research that has examined effective instructional practices for those students with disabilities, who are at risk, and who are struggling in mathematics (see Baker, Gersten, & Lee, 2002; Center on Instruction, 2007; Gersten et al., 2009; Hodge, Riccomini, Buford, & Herbst, 2006; Jayanthi et al., 2008; Maccini, Mulcahy, & Wilson, 2007). The importance of explicit and systematic instruction for low-achieving students should not be overlooked. If the Variable County School District has selected their Tier 1 core mathematics program as a holistic student-centered-only mathematics program, where students must create all of their math knowledge independent of the teacher, then the RTI team should immediately have a plan in place to provide teacher-led explicit instruction for students who struggle, are at-risk, or have a learning disability. Depending on a school's population, if large numbers of students are at risk for various reasons, those students at greatest risk will not have their instructional needs met within the general education curriculum without substantial differentiation from the regular education teacher. The reality may then quickly become an overloaded system with far too many students requiring Tier 2 instructional supports.

It is important to read and react positively to research rather than ignore it. This, however, does not mean it is time to reject all mathematics programs that are based solely on a student-centered instructional approach; of course not. However, it is time to rethink which instructional programs in Tier 1 are selected and to choose programs that meet the needs of the majority of students.

AN ALTERNATIVE APPROACH: A TWO TIER 1 CORE MATHEMATICS PROGRAM

The Two Tier 1 alternative approach (see Figure 10.1) requires the use of two core mathematics programs with one specifically selected for students who are below benchmark (i.e., students at risk, students struggling, and/or students with disabilities). The research results strongly indicate that this program is designed on a teacher-directed approach or a balanced approach. At first

Figure 10.1   The Two Tier 1 Approach to a Mathematics Program

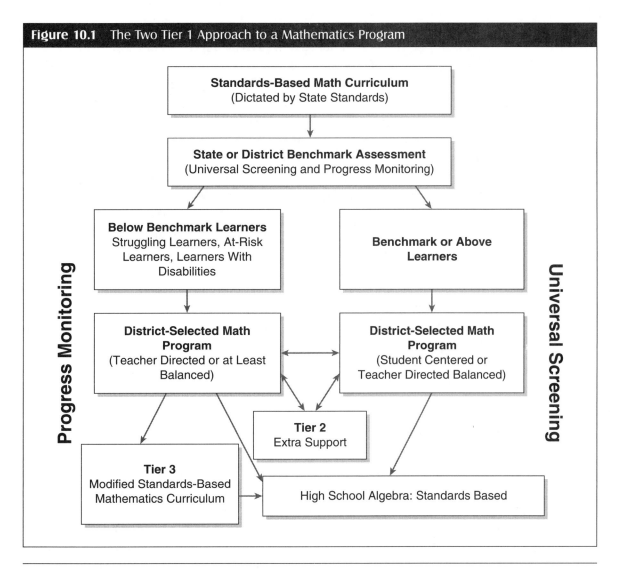

Source: Riccomini, P. J. (2009). *Response to intervention: Implications for math instruction.* Professional Development Session for Educators. Reprinted with permission.

glance, one may view this type of system as returning to the days of "tracking." It is not tracking because both core mathematics programs are addressing parallel state standards with the ultimate goal of mathematical proficiency, albeit one program is addressing the state standards through a teacher-directed instructional approach.

A Two Tier 1 RTI approach does not water down the mathematics standards, but rather takes into consideration the instructional needs of students in the teaching of the standards. In the current system, the main consideration in the selection of a core mathematics program is the alignment with state standards. In this Two Tier 1 approach, both core mathematics curricula were selected based not only on the alignment with state standards but also on student instructional needs, thus ensuring that students receive content aligned with the state standards and a delivery mode necessary for success. Additionally, students are able to move between selected mathematics programs if necessary and warranted by student performance data as well as receive Tier 2 instructional supports as needed. The system is fluid and dynamic, not rigid and set in stone.

As students move through the Two Tier 1 approach, universal screening and progress monitoring are standard as well as teachers' use of the data for instructional decisions. Students that are below benchmark are progress monitored more frequently and provided additional Tier 2 instructional support as needed. Universal screening is also occurring for all students and to make sure no students start to struggle. As with any RTI model, students who are not making progress or adequate progress with Tier 1 and Tier 2 instructional supports may be considered for Tier 3 instructional supports. Using this model, educators are more confident that students' instructional needs were addressed starting in Tier 1 and continuing through Tier 2. This confidence then translates to more accurate decisions regarding eligibility and entitlement for students.

By selecting one core mathematics program, we as an education system are basically saying that this is how everyone should be taught and learn mathematics (even though research shows this is not the case), and if a student by chance struggles, the student must need additional instructional supports. In essence, we are blaming the learners, not the instructional approach (i.e., the curriculum program). This is very different than how schools are setting up their mathematics programs currently and is partially a result of the emphasis placed on state standards as well as logistical issues; but nonetheless, it is an idea for future research and consideration.

SUMMARY

This chapter explored the next steps in the RTI process as models continue to be refined and expanded to secondary settings and to other student groups such as gifted and talented, and included implications for changing systems. We presented an alternative to the current RTI model in math, which generally uses only one core curriculum program for future considerations. Most important, we also called for more research, from both national and local perspectives. As with anything worth doing, an effective RTI model in math will take a great deal of time, energy, and commitment by all involved in the process.

The definition of insanity is doing the same thing over and over and expecting different results.

—Albert Einstein

References

Adams, T. L. (2003). Reading mathematics: More than words can say. *The Reading Teacher, 56*(8), 786–795.

Agodini, R., Harris, B., Atkins-Burnett, S., Heaviside, S., Novak, T., & Murphy, R. (2009). *Achievement effects of four early elementary school math curricula: Findings from first graders in 39 schools* (NCEE 2009-4052). Washington, DC: National Center for Education Evaluation and Regional Assistance, Institute of Education Sciences, U.S. Department of Education.

Allsopp, D. H., Kyger, M. M., & Lovin, L. H. (2007). *Teaching mathematics meaningfully: Solutions for reaching struggling learners.* Baltimore, MD: Paul H. Brookes Publishing Co.

Ardoin, S. P., Witt, J. C., Connell, J. E., & Koenig, J. L. (2001). Application of a three-tier response to intervention model for instructional planning, decision making and the identification of children in need of services. *Journal of Psychoeducational Assessment, 23*(4), 362–380.

Ashlock, R. B. (2006). *Error patterns in computation: Using error patterns to help students learn* (10th ed.). New York: Allyn & Bacon.

Baker, S., Gersten, R., & Lee, D. (2002). A synthesis of empirical research on teaching mathematics to low-achieving students. *The Elementary School Journal, 103,* 51–73.

Baker, S., Gersten, R., & Scanlon, D. (2002). Procedural facilitators and cognitive strategies: Tools for unraveling the mysteries of comprehension and the writing process, and for providing meaningful access to the general curriculum. *Learning Disabilities Research and Practice, 17,* 65–77.

Baker, S. K., Simmons, D. C., & Kame'enui, E. J. (1997). Vocabulary acquisition: Research bases. In D. C. Simmons & E. J. Kame'enui (Eds.), *What reading research tells us about children with diverse learning needs: Bases and basics.* Mahwah, NJ: Erlbaum.

Bryant, D. P., Bryant, B. R., Gersten, R., Scammacca, N., & Chavez, M. M. (2008). Mathematics intervention for first- and second-grade students with mathematics difficulties: The effects of Tier 2 intervention delivered as booster lessons. *Remedial and Special Education, 29,* 20–32.

Butler, F. M., Miller, S. P., Crehan, K., Babbitt, B., & Pierce, T. (2003). Fraction instruction for students with mathematics disabilities: Comparing two teaching sequences. *Learning Disabilities Research and Practice, 18,* 99–111.

Calhoon, M. B., & Fuchs, L. S. (2003). The effects of peer-assisted learning strategies and curriculum-based measurement on the mathematics performance of secondary students with disabilities. *Remedial and Special Education, 24*(4), 235–245.

Carnine, D. W., Silbert, J., Kame'enui, E. J., & Tarver, S. G. (2004). *Direct instruction reading* (3rd ed.). Upper Saddle River, NJ: Merrill/Prentice Hall.

Center on Instruction. (2007). *A synopsis of a synthesis of empirical research on teaching mathematics to low-achieving students.* Portsmouth, NH: RMC Research Corporation: Author.

Crawford, D. B. (2003). *Mastering math facts: Blackline masters and answer keys.* Eau Claire, WI: Otter Creek Institute.

Dehaene, S. (1997). *The number sense: How the mind creates mathematics.* New York: Oxford University Press.

Division for Learning Disabilities. (2007). *Thinking about response to intervention and learning disabilities: A teacher's guide.* Arlington, VA: Author.

Drucker, P. F. (2002). *Managing in the next society.* New York: St. Martin's Press.

Ellis, E. S., Worthington, L., & Larkin, M. J. (1994). *Executive summary of research synthesis on effective teaching principles and the design of quality tools for educators.* (Tech. Rep. No. 6). Retrieved July 17, 2004, from University of Oregon, National Center to Improve the Tools of Educators Web site: http://idea.uoregon.edu/~ncite/ documents/ techrep/other.html.

Foil, C. R., & Alber, S. R. (2002). Fun and effective ways to build your students' vocabulary. *Intervention in School and Clinic, 37*(3), 131–139.

Fuchs, L. S., Compton, D. L., Fuchs, D., Paulsen, K., Bryant, J. D., & Hamlett, C. L. (2005). The prevention, identification, and cognitive determinants of math difficulty. *Journal of Educational Psychology, 97*(3), 493–513.

Fuchs, L. S., & Fuchs, D. (2002). Hot Math: Promoting mathematical problem solving among children with disabilities. *CASL News: Promoting Success in Grades K–3, 7,* 1–4.

Fuchs, L. S., Fuchs, D., Craddock, C., Hollenbeck, K. M., Hamlett, C. L., & Schatschneider, C. (in press). Effects of small-group tutoring with and without validated classroom instruction on at-risk students' math problem solving: Are two tiers of prevention better than one? *Journal of Educational Psychology.*

Fuchs, L. S., Fuchs, D., & Hollenbeck, K. H. (2007). Extending responsiveness to intervention to mathematics at first and third grades. *Learning Disabilities Research & Practice, 22*(1), 13–24.

Fuchs, L. S., Fuchs, D., & Karns, K. (2001). Enhancing kindergarteners' mathematical development: Effects of peer-assisted learning strategies. *Elementary School Journal, 101,* 495–510.

Fuchs, L. S., Fuchs, D., & Prentice, K. (2004). Responsiveness to mathematical problem-solving instruction: Comparing students at risk of mathematics disability with and without risk of reading disability. *Journal of Learning Disabilities, 37*(4), 293–306.

Fuchs, L. S., Fuchs, D., Yazdian, L., Powell, S., & Karns, K. (n.d.). *Peer-assisted learning strategies: First-grade math: Teacher manual.* Available for purchase from Peer-Assisted Learning Strategies Web site: http://www.kc.vanderbilt.edu/kennedy/pals.

Fuchs, L. S., Fuchs, D., Yazdian, L., Powell, S., & Karns, K. (n.d.). *Peer-assisted learning strategies: Kindergarten math: Teacher manual.* Available for purchase from Peer-Assisted Learning Strategies Web site: http://www.kc.vanderbilt.edu/kennedy/pals.

Fuchs, L. S., Seethaler, P. M., Powell, S. R., Fuchs, D., Hamlett, C. L., & Fletcher, J. M. (2008). Effects of preventative tutoring on the mathematical problem solving of third-grade students with risk for math and reading disabilities. *Exceptional Children, 74* (2), 155–173.

Geary, D. C. (2004). Mathematics and learning disabilities. *Journal of Learning Disabilities, 37,* 4–15.

Geary, D. C., Hoard, M. K., & Hamson, C. O. (1999). Numerical and arithmetical cognition: Patterns of functions and deficits in children at risk for a mathematical disability. *Journal of Experimental Child Psychology, 74*(3), 213–239.

Gersten, R., Beckmann, S., Clarke, B., Foegen, A., Marsh, L., Star, J. R., & Witzel, B. (2009). *Assisting students struggling with mathematics: Response to Intervention (RTI) for elementary and middle schools* (NCEE 2009-4060). Washington, DC: National Center for Education Evaluation and Regional Assistance, Institute of Education Sciences, U.S. Department of Education. Retrieved from http://ies.ed.gov/ncee/wwc/publications/practiceguides.

Gersten, R., & Chard, D. J. (1999). Number sense: Rethinking math instruction for students with learning disabilities. *Journal of Special Education, 33*, 18–28.

Gersten, R., Clarke, B. S., & Jordan, N. C. (2007). *Screening for mathematics difficulties in K–3 students.* Portsmouth, NH: RMC Research Corporation, Center on Instruction.

Hall, E. K. (2008). *A principal's guide: Implementing response to intervention.* Thousand Oaks, CA: Corwin.

Hodge, J., Riccomini, P. J., Buford, R., & Herbst, M. (2006). A review of instructional interventions in mathematics for students with emotional and behavioral disorders. *Behavioral Disorders, 31*(3), 297–311.

Hoover, J. H. (2009). *RTI: Assessment essentials for struggling learners.* Thousand Oaks, CA: Corwin.

Hosp, M. K., Hosp, J. L., & Howell, K. W. (2007). *The ABCs of CBM: A practical guide to curriculum-based measurement.* New York: Guilford Press.

Hutchinson, N. L. (1993). Second invited response: Students with disabilities and mathematics education reform—let the dialog begin. *Remedial and Special Education, 14*(6), 20–23.

IRIS Center for Training Enhancements. (n.d.). *Algebra (part 1): Applying learning strategies to beginning algebra.* Retrieved on March 5, 2007, from http://iris.peabody.vanderbilt.edu.

IRIS Center for Training Enhancements. (n.d.). *Algebra (part 2): Applying learning strategies to intermediate algebra.* Retrieved on March 5, 2007, from http://iris.peabody.vanderbilt.edu.

IRIS Center for Training Enhancements. (n.d.). *Comprehension & vocabulary: Grades 3–5.* Retrieved on March 5, 2007, from http://iris.peabody.vanderbilt.edu.

IRIS Center for Training Enhancements. (n.d.). *Effective room arrangement.* Retrieved on March 5, 2007, from http://iris.peabody.vanderbilt.edu/gpm/chalcycle.htm.

Ives, B., & Hoy, C. (2003). Graphic organizers applied to higher-level secondary mathematics. *Learning Disabilities Research & Practice, 18*(1), 36–51.

Jayanthi, M., Gersten, R., & Baker, S. (2008). *Mathematics instruction for students with learning disabilities or difficulty learning mathematics: A guide for teachers.* Portsmouth, NH: RMC Research Corporation, Center on Instruction.

Jitendra, A. K. (2002). Teaching students math problem solving through graphic representations. *Teaching Exceptional Children, 34*(4), 34–38.

Jitendra, A. K. (2007). *Solving math word problems: Teaching students with learning disabilities using schema-based instruction.* Austin, TX: PRO-ED, Inc.

Jitendra, A. K., & Hoff, K. (1996). The effects of schema-based instruction on mathematical problem solving performance of students with learning disabilities. *Journal of Learning Disabilities, 29*(4), 422–431.

Jones, C. J. (2001). CBAs that work: Assessing students' math content-reading levels. *Teaching Exceptional Children, 34*(1), 24–28.

Jordan, L., Miller, M. D., & Mercer, C. D. (1999). The effects of concrete to semi-concrete to abstract instruction in the acquisition and retention of fraction concepts and skills. *Learning Disabilities: A Multidisciplinary Journal, 9*, 115–122.

Jordan, N. C., Kaplan, D., Locuniak, M. N., & Ramineni, C. (2007). Predicting first grade math achievement from developmental number sense trajectories. *Learning Disabilities Research and Practice, 22*(1), 36–46.

Jordan, N. C., Kaplan, D., Ramineni, C., & Locuniak, M. N. (2008). Development of number combination skill in the early school years: When do fingers help? *Developmental Science, 11,* 662–668.

Kroesbergen, E. H., & Van Luit, J. E. H. (2003). Mathematic interventions for children with special educational needs: A meta-analysis. *Remedial and Special Education, 24*(2), 97–114.

Locuniak, M. N., & Jordan, N. C. (2008). Using kindergarten number sense to predict calculation fluency in second grade. *Journal of Learning Disabilities, 41,* 451–459.

Maccini, P., & Gagnon, J. C. (2000). Best practices for teaching mathematics to secondary students with special needs. *Focus on Exceptional Children, 32*(5), 1–21.

Maccini, P., & Hughes, C. A. (2000). Effects of a problem-solving strategy on the introductory algebra performance of secondary students with learning disabilities. *Learning Disabilities Research and Practice, 15*(1), 10–21.

Maccini, P., Mulcahy, C. A., & Wilson, M. G. (2007). A follow-up of mathematics interventions for secondary students with learning disabilities. *Learning Disabilities Research & Practice, 22*(1), 58–74.

Mellard, D. F., & Johnson, E. (2008). *RTI: A practitioner's guide to implementing response to intervention.* Thousand Oaks, CA: Corwin.

Miller, S. P., & Mercer, C. D. (1993). Using data to learn about concrete-semiconcrete-abstract instruction for students with math disabilities. *Learning Disabilities Research & Practice, 8,* 89–96.

National Association of State Directors of Special Education. (2006). *Response to intervention: A joint paper by the National Association of State Directors of Special Education and the Council of Administrators of Special Education.* Retrieved December 15, 2008, from www.nasdse.org/projects.

National Council of Teachers of Mathematics. (2000). *Principles and standards for school mathematics.* Reston, VA: Author.

National Council of Teachers of Mathematics. (2006). *Curriculum focal points for mathematics in prekindergarten through Grade 8 mathematics.* Reston, VA: Author.

National Mathematics Advisory Panel (NMAP). (2008). *Foundations for success: The final report of the National Mathematics Advisory Panel.* U.S. Department of Education Washington, DC. Retrieved March 2008 from www.ed.gov/MathPanel.

National Research Council. (2001). In J. Kilpatrick, J. Swafford, & B. Findell (Eds.), *Adding it up: Helping children learn mathematics.* Mathematics Learning Study Committee, Center for Education, Division of Behavioral and Social Sciences and Education. Washington, DC: National Academy Press.

Newman-Gonchar, R., Clarke, B., & Gersten, R. (2009). *A summary of nine key studies: Multitier intervention and response to interventions for students struggling in mathematics.* Portsmouth, NH: RMC Research Corporation, Center on Instruction. Retrieved February 1, 2009, from www.centeroninstruction.com.

Owen, R. L., & Fuchs, L. S. (2002). Mathematical problem-solving strategy instruction for third-grade students with learning disabilities. *Remedial and Special Education, 23,* 268–278.

Phillips, N. B., Fuchs, L. S., & Fuchs, D. (1994). Effects of classwide curriculum-based measurement and peer tutoring: A collaborative researcher-practitioner interview study. *Journal of Learning Disabilities, 27,* 420–434.

Pierangelo, R., & Giuliani, G. (2008). *Frequently asked questions about response to intervention.* Thousand Oaks, CA: Corwin.

Raiker, A. (2002). Spoken language and mathematics. *Cambridge Journal of Education, 32*(1), 45–60.

Riccomini, P. J. (2005). Identification and remediation of systematic error patterns in subtraction. *Learning Disability Quarterly, 28*(3), 1–10.

Riccomini, P. J., Sanders, S., & Jones, J. (2008). The key to enhancing students' mathematical vocabulary knowledge. *Journal of School Educational Technology, 4*(1), 1–7.

Riccomini, P. J., & Witzel, B. S. (2009). *Computation of integers: Math intervention for elementary and middle grades students.* Upper Saddle River, NJ: Pearson Education, Inc.

Riccomini, P. J., Witzel, B. S., & Riccomini, A. E. (in press). Maximize development in early childhood math programs by optimizing the instructional sequence. In N. L. Gallenstein & J. Hodges (Eds.), *Mathematics for all.* Olney, MD: ACEI.

Rubenstein, R. N. (2000). Word origins: Building communication, connections. *Mathematics Teaching in Middle School, 5,* 493–498.

Sanders, S., Riccomini, P. J., & Witzel, B. S. (2005). The algebra readiness of high school students in South Carolina: Implications for middle school math teachers. *South Carolina Middle School Journal, 13,* 45–47.

Schwartzman, S. (1994). *The words of mathematics: An etymological dictionary of mathematical terms used in English.* Washington, DC: Mathematical Association of America.

Seethaler, P. M., Powell, S. R., & Fuchs, L. S. (n.d.). Help students solve problems with "pirate math." *Council for Exceptional Children.* Retrieved January 15, 2009, from www.cec.sped.org.

Shores, C., & Chester, K. (2009). *Using RTI for school improvement: Raising every student's achievement scores.* Thousand Oaks, CA: Corwin.

Simon, R., & Hanrahan, J. P. (2004, June). An evaluation of the Touch Math method for teaching addition to students with learning disabilities. *European Journal of Special Needs Education, 19*(2), 191–209.

Stecker, P. M., Fuchs, L. S., & Fuchs, D. (2005). Using curriculum-based measurement to improve student achievement: Review of research. *Psychology in the Schools, 42*(8), 795–819.

Stein, M., Kinder, D., Silbert, J., & Carnine, D. (2006). *Designing effective mathematics instruction: A direct instruction approach* (4th ed.). Upper Saddle River, NJ: Pearson Education, Inc.

Tournaki, N. (2003). The differential effects of teaching addition through strategy instruction versus drill and practice to students with and without disabilities. *Journal of Learning Disabilities, 36,* 449–458.

VanDerHeyden, A. M., & Burns, M. K. (2005). Using curriculum-based assessment and curriculum-based measurement to guide elementary mathematics instruction: Effect on individual and group accountability scores. *Assessment for Effective Intervention, 30*(3), 15–31.

VanDerHeyden, A. M., Witt, J. C., & Gilbertson, D. (2007). A multi-year evaluation of the effects of an RTI model on identification of children for special education. *Journal of School Psychology, 45*(20), 225–256.

Wilmon, B. (1971). Reading in the content area: A new math terminology list for the primary grades. *Elementary English, 48,* 463–471.

Wilson, C. L., & Sindelar, P. T. (1991). Direct instruction in math word problems: Students with learning disabilities. *Exceptional Children, 57,* 512–518.

Witzel, B. S. (2005). Using CRA to teach algebra to students with math difficulties in inclusive settings. *Learning Disabilities: A Contemporary Journal, 3*(2), 49–60.

Witzel, B. S. (2009). *Response to intervention in mathematics: Strategies for success.* Peterborough, NH: Staff Development for Educators.

Witzel, B. S., Mercer, C. D., & Miller, M. D. (2003). Teaching algebra to students with learning difficulties: An investigation of an explicit instruction model. *Learning Disabilities Research and Practice, 18,* 121–131.

Witzel, B. S., & Riccomini, P. J. (2007). OPTIMIZE your curriculum for students with disabilities. *Preventing School Failure, 52*(1), 13–18.

Witzel, B. S., & Riccomini, P. J. (2009). *Computation of fractions: Math interventions for elementary and middle grades students.* Upper Saddle River, NJ: Pearson Education, Inc.

Xin, Y. P., Jitendra, A. K., & Deatline-Buchman, A. (2005). Effects of mathematical word problem-solving instruction on middle school students with learning problems. *Journal of Special Education, 39*, 181–192.

Index

CORWIN
A SAGE Company